Funeral
Sermons
and
Outlines

F. B. Meyer

PULPIT LIBRARY

BAKER BOOK HOUSE Grand Rapids, Michigan 49506

PREFACE

The preparation of the funeral sermon or address is one of the most exacting duties of the
minister. The environing atmosphere of one
death has certain elements in common with that
of all other deaths. And these common charac-
teristics are such as to call for the greatest care
in preparing an appropriate message. The minister's task is made doubly difficult by the fact
that every death is individual and is attended by
its own peculiar circumstances and effects. These
are the considerations which have guided the assembling of the material for this volume.

This book is a handbook for use in preparing
funeral sermons or addresses. It includes complete sermons, condensed sermons, outlines, quo-
table poetry, pertinent illustrations and quota-
tions, select hymns, and suggested themes and
texts. These selections are gleaned from the
writings of the sermon masters of yesteryears.

THE PUBLISHERS.

CONTENTS

I. Complete Sermons

The Death of Death

F. B. MEYER

*Forasmuch then as the children are partakers of flesh
and blood, he also himself likewise took part of the
same; that through death he might destroy him that had
the power of death, that is, the devil; and deliver them,
who through fear of death were all their lifetime subject to bondage.* — HEB. 2:14, 15.

W E fear death with a double fear. There is, first *the instinc-
tive fear* shared also by the animal creation; for the very
brutes tremble as the moment of death draws near. Surely this
fear is not wrong. It is often congenital and involuntary, and
afflicts some of God's noblest saints: though doubtless these will
some day confess that it was most unwarrantable, and that the
moment of dissolution was calm and sweet and blessed.

It is a growing opinion among thoughtful men that the moment of death, when the spirit passes from its earthly tabernacle, is probably the most painless and the happiest moment of
its whole earthly story. And if this be so generally, how much
more must it be the case with those on whose sight are break-
ing the glories of Paradise! The child whose eyes feast upon a
flowing vista of flower and fruit, beckoning it through the gar-
den-gate, hardly notices the rough woodwork of the gate itself
as it bounds through; and probably the soul, becoming aware
of the beauty of the king and the glories of its home, is too ab-
sorbed to notice the act of death, till it suddenly finds itself free
to mount and soar and revel in the dawning light.

But there is another fear of death, which is *spiritual. We
dread its mystery.* What is it? Whither does it lead? Why does
it come just now? What is the nature of the life beyond? We
see the movements on the other side of the thick curtain which
sways to and fro; but we can distinguish no form. The dying
ones are conscious of sights and sounds for which we strain eye
and ear in vain.

We dread its leave-taking. — The heathen poet sang sadly of leaving earth and home and family. Long habit endears the homeliest lot and the roughest comrades: how much more the true-hearted and congenial. If only we could all go together, there would be nothing in it. But this separate dropping-off, this departing one by one, this drift from the anchorage alone! Who can deny that it is a lonesome thing?

Men dread the after-death. — "The sting of death is sin." The sinner dreads to die, because he knows that, on the other side of death, he must meet the God against whom he has sinned, and stand at his bar to give an account and receive the due reward of his deeds. How can he face that burning glory? How can he answer for one of a thousand? How can mortal man be just with God? How can he escape hell, and find his place amid the happy festal throngs of the Golden City?

Many of man's fears were known to Christ. And he knew that they would be felt by many who were to be closely related to him as brethren. If, then, he was prompted by ordinary feelings of compassion to the great masses of mankind, he would be especially moved to relieve those with whom he had so close an affinity, as these marvelous verses unfold. He and they are all of one (vs. 11). He calls them brethren through the lips of psalmist and prophet (vs. 12). He takes his stand in the assembled Church, and sings his Father's praise in its company (vs. 12). He even associates himself with them in their humble childlike trust (vs. 13). He dares to accost the gaze of all worlds, as he comes forward leading them by the hand (vs. 13). Oh, marvelous identification! Oh, rapturous association! More wondrous far than if a seraph should cherish friendship with a worm! But the preciousness of this relationship lies in the fact that Jesus will do all he can to alleviate that fear of death, which is more or less common to us all.

But in order to do it, he must die. He could not be the death of death unless he had personally tasted death. He needed to fulfill the law of death by dying, before he could abolish death. Our David must go into the valley of Elah, and grapple with our giant foe, and wrest from him his power, and slay him with his own sword. As in the old fable Prometheus could not slay the Minotaur unless he accompanied the yearly freight of victims, so must Jesus go with the myriads of our race into the dark confines of the tomb, that death may do its worst in vain; that the grave may lose its victory; and that the grim jailer may be shown powerless to hold the Resurrection and the life. Had Christ not died, it might have been affirmed that, in one place at least, death and sin, chaos and darkness, were supreme. "It behooved him, therefore, to suffer, and to rise from the dead the third day." And, like another Samson, carrying the gates of his prison-house, he came forth, demonstrating forever that light is stronger than darkness, salvation than sin, life than death. Hear his triumphant cry, as thrice the risen and ascended Master exclaims, "I died, and lo, I am alive forevermore, and have the keys of Hades and of death." Death and hell chose their own battleground — their strongest; and there, in the hour of his weakness, our King defeated them, and now carries the trophy of victory at his girdle forevermore. Hallelujah!

But he could only have died by becoming man. — Perhaps there is no race in the universe that can die but our own. So there may be no other spot in the wide universe of God seamed with graves, shadowed by the outspread wings of the angel of death, or marked by the plague-spot of sin. "Sin entered into the world, and death by sin; and so death passed upon all." In order then to die, Christ must take on himself our human nature. Others die because they are born; Christ was born that he might die. It is as if he said: "Of thee, O human mother, must I be born; and I must suffer the aches and pains and sorrows of mortal life! and I must hasten quickly to the destined goal of human life; I have come into the world to die." "Forasmuch as the children are partakers of flesh and blood, he also himself likewise took part of the same, *in order that* through death he might destroy him that had the power of death, that is, the devil: and deliver them, who through fear of death were all their lifetime subject to bondage."

BY DEATH CHRIST DESTROYED HIM THAT HAD THE POWER OF DEATH. Scripture has no doubt as to the existence of the devil. And those who know much of their own inner life, and of the sudden assaults of evil to which we are liable, cannot but realize his terrible power. And from this passage we infer that that power was even greater before Jesus died. "He had the power of death." It was a chief weapon in his infernal armory. The dread of it was so great as to drive men to yield to any demands made by the priests of false religions, with their dark impurities and hideous rites. Thus timid sheep are scared by horrid shouts and blows into the butcher's shambles.

But since Jesus died, the devil and his power are destroyed; brought to naught, not made extinct. Still he assails the Christian warrior, though armed from head to foot; and goes about seeking whom he may devour, and deceives men to ruin. Satan is not impotent though chained. He has received the wound which annuls his power, but it has not yet been effectual to destroy him.

His power was broken at the cross and grave of Jesus. The hour of Gethsemane was the hour and power of darkness. And Satan must have seen the Resurrection in despair. It was the knell of his destiny. It sealed his doom. The prince of this world was judged and cast out from the seat of power (John 12:31; 16:11). The serpent's head was bruised beyond remedy.

Fear not the devil, O child of God; nor death! These make much noise, but they have no power. The Breaker has gone before thee, clearing the way. Only keep close behind him. Hark! He gives thee power over all the power of the enemy, and nothing shall by any means hurt thee (Luke 10:19). No robber shall pluck thee from thy Shepherd's hand.

BY DEATH CHRIST DELIVERS FROM THE FEAR OF DEATH. A child was in the habit of playing in a large and beautiful garden, with sunny lawns; but there was one part of it, a long and winding path, down which he never ventured; indeed, he dreaded to go near it because some silly nurse had told him that ogres and goblins dwelt within its darksome gloom. At last his eldest brother heard of his fear, and, after playing one day with him, took him to the embowered entrance of the grove, and, leaving him there terror-stricken, went singing through its length, and returned, and reasoned with the child, proving that his fears were groundless. At last he took the lad's hand, and they went through it together. From that moment the fear which had haunted the place fled. And the memory of that brother's presence took its place. So has Jesus done for us!

Fear not the mystery of death! Jesus has died, and has shown us that it is the gateway into another life, more fair and blessed than this — a life in which human words are understood, and human faces smile, and human affections linger still. The forty days of his resurrection life have solved many of the problems, and illumined most of the mystery. To die is to go at once to be with him. No chasm, no interval, no weary delay in purgatory. Absent from the body, present with the Lord. One moment here in conditions of mortality; the next beyond the stars.

Fear not the loneliness of death! The soul in the dark valley becomes aware of another at its side, "Thou art with me." Death cannot separate us, even for a moment, from the love of God, which is in Christ Jesus our Lord. In the hour of death Jesus fulfills his own promise, "I will come again and take you unto myself." And on the other side we step into a vast circle of loving spirits, who welcome the newcomer with festal songs (II Peter 1:11).

Fear not the after-death! — The curse and penalty of sin have been borne by him. Death, the supreme sentence on sinners, has been suffered for us by our Substitute. In him we have indeed passed on to the other side of the doom, which is justly ours, as members of a sinful race. "Who is he that condemneth? It is Christ that died, yea, rather, that is risen again."

Death! How shall they die who have already died in Christ? That which others call *death,* we call *sleep.* We dread it no more than sleep. Our bodies lie down exhausted with the long working-day, to awake in the fresh energy of the eternal morning; but in the meanwhile the spirit is presented faultless before the presence of his glory with exceeding joy.

Pictures of Life

CHARLES H. SPURGEON

What is your life? — JAMES 4:14.

I T well behooves me, now that another year of my existence has
almost gone, standing on the threshold of a fresh era, to consider what I am, where I am going, what I am doing, whom I
am serving, and what shall be my reward. I will not, however,
do so publicly before you; I hope that I may be enabled to perform that duty in secret; but rather let me turn this occurrence
to another account by speaking to you of the frailty of human
life, the fleeting nature of time, how swiftly it passes away, how
soon we all shall fade as a leaf, and how speedily the place which
knows us now shall know us no more for ever. The apostle
James asks, "What is your life?" and, thanks to inspiration, we
are at no great difficulty to give the reply; for Scripture being
the best interpreter of Scripture, supplies us with many very excellent answers. I shall attempt to give you some of them.

1. First, we shall view life with regard to ITS SWIFTNESS.

It is a great fact that though life to the young man, when
viewed in the prospect appears to be long, to the old man, it is
ever short, and to all men life is really but a brief period. Human life is not long. Compare it with the existence of some animals and trees, and how short is human life! Compare it with
the ages of the universe, and it becomes a span; and especially
measure it by eternity, and how little does life appear! It sinks
like one small drop into the ocean, and becomes as insignificant as
one tiny grain of sand upon the seashore.

Life is swift. If you would picture life, you must turn to the
Bible, and this evening we will walk through the Bible-gallery of
old paintings.

You will find its swiftness spoken of in the Book of Job, where
we are furnished with three illustrations. In the ninth chapter
and at the twenty-fifth verse, we read, "Now my days are *swifter
than a post.*" We are most of us acquainted with the swiftness
of modern post-conveyance. But since, in this ancient Book,
there can be no allusion to modern posts, we must turn to the

12

manners and customs of the East, and in so doing we find that
the ancient monarchs astonished their subjects by the amazing
rapidity with which they received intelligence. By well-ordered
arrangements, swift horses, and constant relays, they were able
to attain a speed which, although trifling in these days, was in
those slower ages a marvel of marvels; so that, to an Eastern,
one of the clearest ideas of swiftness was that of "a post." Well
doth Job say that our life is swifter than a post. We ride one
year until it is worn out, but there comes another just as swift,
and we are borne by it, and soon it is gone, and another year
serves us for a steed; post-house after post-house we pass, as
birthdays successively arrive; we loiter not, but vaulting at a
leap from one year to another, still we hurry onward, onward,
ever onward. My life is like a post; not like the slow wagon
that drags along the road with tiresome wheels, but like a post,
it attains the greatest speed.

Job further says, "My days are passed away *as the swift
ships.*" He increases, you see, the intensity of the metaphor; for
if, in the Eastern's idea, anything could exceed the swiftness
of the post, it was the swift ship. Some translate this passage,
"as the ships of desire"; that is, the ships hurrying home, anxious for the haven, and therefore crowding on all sail. You may
well conceive how swiftly the mariner flies from a threatening
storm, or seeks the port where he will find his home. You have
sometimes seen how the ship cuts through the billows, leaving
a white furrow behind her, and causing the sea to boil around
her. Such is life, says Job, "as the swift ships," when the sails
are filled by the wind, and the vessel dashes on, cleaving a passage through the crowding waves. Swift are the ships, but swifter
far is life. The wind of time bears me along. I cannot stop its
motion; I may direct it with the rudder of God's Holy Spirit; I
may, it is true, take in some small sails of sin, which might hurry
my days on faster than otherwise they would go; but, nevertheless, like a swift ship, my life must speed on its way until it
reaches its haven. Where is that haven to be? Shall it be found
in the land of bitterness and barrenness, that dreary region of
the lost? Or shall it be that sweet haven of eternal peace, where
not a troubling wave can ruffle the quiescent glory of my spirit?
Wherever the haven is to be, that truth is the same, we are "as
the swift ships."

Job also says that life is *as the eagle that hasteth to the prey.*"
The eagle is a bird noted for its swiftness. I remember reading

an account of an eagle attacking a fish-hawk, which had obtained some booty from the deep, and was bearing it aloft. The hawk dropped the fish, which fell towards the water; but before the fish had reached the ocean, the eagle had flown more swiftly than the fish could fall, and catching it in its beak it flew away with it. The swiftness of the eagle is almost incalculable; you see it, and it is gone; you see a dark speck in the sky yonder; it is an eagle soaring; let the fowler imagine that, by-and-by, he shall overtake it on some mountain's craggy peak, it shall be gone long before he reaches it. Such is our life. It is like an eagle hasting to its prey; not merely an eagle flying in its ordinary course, but an eagle hasting to its prey. Life appears to be hasting to its end; death seeks the body as its prey; life is ever fleeing from insatiate death; but death is too swift to be outrun, and as an eagle overtakes his prey, so shall death.

If we require a further illustration of the swiftness of life, we must turn to two other passages in the Book of Job, upon which I shall not dwell. One will be found in the seventh chapter, at the sixth verse, where Job says, "My days are *swifter than a weaver's shuttle*," which the weaver throws so quickly that the eye can hardly discern it. But he gives us a yet more excellent metaphor in the seventh verse of the same chapter, where he says, "O remember that *my life is wind*." Now this excels in velocity all the other figures we have examined. Who can outstride the winds? Proverbially, the winds are rapid; even in their gentlest motion they appear to be swift. But when they rush in the tornado, or when they dash madly on in the hurricane, when the tempest blows, and tears down everything, how swift is the wind! Perhaps some of us may have a gentle gale of wind, and we may not seem to move so swiftly; but with others, who are only just born, and then snatched away to heaven, the swiftness may be compared to that of the hurricane, which soon snaps the ties of life, and leaves the infant dead. Surely our life is like the wind.

Oh! if you could but catch these ideas, my friends! Though we may be sitting still in this chapel, yet you know that we are all really in motion. This world is turning round on its axis once in four-and-twenty hours; and besides that, it is moving round the sun in the 365 days of the year. So that we are all moving, we are all flitting along through space; and as we are travelling through space, so are we moving through time at an incalculable rate. Oh, what an idea this is, could we but grasp it!

We are all being carried along as if by a giant angel, with broad outstretched wings, which he flaps to the blast, and flying before the lightning, makes us ride on the winds. The whole multitude of us are hurrying along, — whither, remains to be decided by the test of our faith and the grace of God; but certain it is that we are all travelling. Do not think that you are stable, fixed in one position; fancy not that you are standing still; you are not. Your pulses each moment beat the funeral marches to the tomb. You are chained to the chariot of rolling time; there is no bridling the steeds, or leaping from the chariot; you must be constantly in motion.

Thus, then, have I spoken of the swiftness of life.

2. But, next, I must speak concerning THE UNCERTAINTY OF LIFE, of which we have abundant illustrations.

Let us refer to that part of Scripture from which I have chosen my text, the Epistle of James, the fourth chapter, at the fourteenth verse: "For what is your life? It is even a *vapour,* that appeareth for a little time, and then vanisheth away." If I were to ask for a child's explanation of this, I know what he would say. He would say, "Yes, it is even a vapour, like a bubble that is blown upward." Children sometimes blow bubbles, and amuse themselves thereby. Life is even as that bubble. You see it rising into the air; the child delights in seeing it fly about, but it is all gone in one moment. "It is even a vapour, that appeareth for a little time, and then vanisheth away." But if you ask the poet to explain this, he would tell you that, in the morning, sometimes at early dawn, the rivers send up a steamy offering to the sun. There is a vapour, a mist, an exhalation rising from the rivers and brooks; but in a very little while after the sun has risen all that mist has gone. Hence we read of "the morning cloud, and the early dew that passeth away." A more common observer, speaking of a vapour, would think of those thin clouds you sometimes see floating in the air, which are so light that they are soon carried away. Indeed, a poet uses them as the picture of feebleness, —

> "Their hosts are scatter'd, like thin clouds
> Before a Biscay gale."

The wind moves them, and they are gone, "What is your life? It is even a vapour, that appeareth for a little time, and then vanisheth away." So uncertain is life!

Again, if you read in the Book of Ecclesiastes, at the sixth chapter, and the twelfth verse, you will there find life compared to something else, even more fragile than a vapour. The wise man there says that it is even "as *a shadow*." Now, what can there be less substantial than a shadow? What substance is there in a shadow? Who can lay hold of it? You may see a person's shadow as he passes you, but the moment the person passes away his shadow is gone. Yea, and who can grasp his life? Many men reckon upon a long existence, and think they are going to live here for ever; but who can calculate upon a shadow? Go, thou foolish man, who sayest to thy soul, "Thou hast much goods laid up for many years; take thine ease, eat, drink, and be merry"; go thou, and store thy room with shadows; go thou, and pile up shadows, and say, "These are mine, and they shall never depart." But thou sayest, "I cannot catch a shadow." No, and thou canst not reckon on a year, or even a moment, for it is a shadow, that soon melteth away, and is gone.

King Hezekiah also furnishes us with a simile, where he says that life is *as a thread which is cut off*. You will find this in the prophecy of Isaiah, the thirty-eighth chapter, at the twelfth verse: "Mine age is departed, and is removed from me as a shepherd's tent: I have cut off like a weaver my life." The weaver cuts off his thread very easily, and so is life soon ended.

I might continue my illustration at pleasure concerning the uncertainty of life. We might find, perhaps, a score more figures in Scripture if we would search. Take, for instance, the grass, the flowers of the field, etc.

But though life is swift, and though it is to pass away so speedily we are still generally very anxious to know what it is to be while we have it. For we say, if we are to lose it soon, still, while we live, let us live; and whilst we are to be here, be it ever so short a time, let us know what we are to expect in it.

3. And that leads us, in the third place, to look at LIFE IN ITS CHANGES.

If you want pictures of the changes of life, turn to this wonderful Book of poetry, the Sacred Scriptures, and there you will find metaphors piled on metaphors. And, first, you will find life compared to *a pilgrimage* by good old Jacob, in the forty-seventh chapter of Genesis, and the ninth verse. That hoary-headed patriarch, when he was asked by Pharaoh what was his age, replied, "The days of the years of *my pilgrimage* are an hundred and thirty years; few and evil have the days of the years of my life been, and have not attained unto the days of the years of the life of my fathers in the days of their pilgrimage." He calls life a pilgrimage. A pilgrim sets out in the morning, and he has to journey many a day before he gets to the shrine which he seeks. What varied scenes the traveller will behold on his way! Sometimes he will be on the mountains, anon he will descend into the valleys; here he will be where the brooks shine like silver, where the birds warble, where the air is balmy, and the trees are green, and luscious fruits hang down to gratify his taste; anon he will find himself in the arid desert, where no life is found, and no sound is heard, except the screech of the wild eagle in the air, where he finds no rest for the sole of his foot, — the burning sky above him, and the hot sand beneath him, — no roof-tree, and no house to rest himself; at another time he finds himself in a sweet oasis, resting himself by the wells of water, and plucking fruit from palm-trees. At one time he walks between the rocks, in some narrow gorge, where all is darkness; at another time he ascends the hill Mizar; now he descends into the valley of Baca; anon he climbs the hill of Bashan, and a high hill is the hill Bashan; and yet again going into the mountains of leopards, he suffers trial and affliction.

Such is life, ever changing. Who can tell what may come next? Today it is fair, tomorrow there may be the thundering storm; today I may want for nothing, tomorrow I may be like Jacob, with nothing but a stone for my pillow, and the heavens for my curtains. But what a happy thought it is; though we know not how the road winds, we know where it ends. It is the straightest way to heaven to go round about. Israel's forty years' wanderings were, after all, the nearest path to Canaan. We may have to go through trial and affliction; the pilgrimage may be a tiresome one, but it is safe; we cannot trace the river upon which we are sailing, but we know it ends in floods of bliss at last. We cannot track the roads, but we know that they all meet in the great metropolis of heaven, in the center of God's universe. God help us to pursue the true pilgrimage of a pious life!

We have another picture of life in its changes given to us in the ninetieth Psalm, at the ninth verse: "We spend our years *as a tale that is told.*" Now David understood about tales that were told; I daresay he had been annoyed by them sometimes, and amused by them at other times. There are, in the East, professed storytellers, who amuse their hearers by inventing tales such as those in that foolish book, the "Arabian Nights." When I was foolish enough to read that book, I remember sometimes you were with fairies, sometimes with genii, sometimes in palaces, anon you went down into caverns. All sorts of singular things are conglomerated into what they call a tale. Now, says David, "we spend our years as a tale that is told." You know there is nothing so wonderful as the history of the odds and ends of human life. Sometimes it is a merry rhyme, sometimes a prosy subject; sometimes you ascend to the sublime, soon you descend to the ridiculous. No man can write the whole of his own biography; I suppose, if the complete history of a man's thoughts and words could be written, the world itself would hardly contain the record, so wonderful is the tale that might be told. Our lives are all singular, and must to ourselves seem strange; of which much might be said. Our life is "as a tale that is told."

Another idea we get from the thirty-eighth chapter of the prophecy of Isaiah, at the twelfth verse: "I am removed *as a shepherd's tent*." The shepherds in the East build temporary huts near the sheep, which are soon removed when the flock moves on; when the hot season comes on, they pitch their tents in the most favorable place they can find, and each season has its suitable position. My life is like a shepherd's tent. I have pitched my tent in a variety of places already; but where I shall pitch it by-and-by, I do not know, I cannot tell. Present probabilities seem to say that —

> "Here I shall make my settled rest,
>   And neither go nor come;
> No more a stranger or a guest,
>   But like a child at home."

But I cannot tell, and you cannot divine. I know that my tent cannot be removed till God says, "Go Forward"; and it cannot stand firm unless he makes it so.

> "All my ways shall ever be
> Order'd by his wise decree."

You have been opening a new shop lately, and you are thinking of settling down in trade, and managing a thriving concern; now paint not the future too brightly, do not be too sure as to what is in store for you. Another has for a long time been engaged in an old establishment; your father always carried on trade there, and you have no thought of moving; but here you have no abiding city; your life is like a shepherd's tent; you may be here, there, and almost everywhere before you die. It was once said by Solon, "No man ought to be called a happy man till he dies," because he does not know what his life is to be;

but Christians may always call themselves happy men here, because, wherever their tent is carried, they cannot pitch it where the cloud does not move, and where they are not surrounded by a circle of fire. God will be a wall of fire round about them, and their glory in the midst. They cannot dwell where God is not the bulwark of their salvation.

If any of you who are God's people are going to change your condition, are going to move out of one situation into another, to take a new business, or remove to another county, you need not fear; God was with you in the last place, and he will be with you in this. He hath said, "Fear thou not; for I am with thee: be not dismayed; for I am thy God." That is an oft-told story of Caesar in a storm. The sailors were all afraid; but he exclaimed, "Fear not! thou carriest Caesar and all his fortunes." So is it with the poor Christian. There is a storm coming on, but fear not, thou art carrying Jesus, and thou must sink or swim with him. Well may any true believer say, "Lord, if thou art with me, it matters not where my tent is. All must be well, though my life is removed like a shepherd's tent."

Again, our life is compared in the Psalms to *a dream*. Now, if a tale is singular, surely a dream is still more so. If a tale is changing and shifting, what is a dream? As for dreams, those flutterings of the benighted fancy, those revelries of the imagination, who can tell what they consist of? We dream of everything in the world, and a few things more! If we were asked to tell our dreams, it would be impossible for us to do so. You dream that you are at a feast; and lo! the viands change into Pegasus, and you are riding through the air; or, again, suddenly transformed into a morsel for a monster's meal. Such is life. The changes occur as suddenly as they happen in a dream. Men have been rich one day, and they have been beggars the next. We have witnessed the exile of monarchs, and the flight of a potentate; or, in another direction, we have seen a man, neither reputable in company nor honorable in station, at a single stride exalted to a throne; and you, who would have shunned him in the street before, were foolish enough to throng your thoroughfares to stare at him. Ah! such is life. Leaves of the Sibyl were not more easily moved by the winds, nor are dreams more variable. "Boast not thyself of tomorrow; for thou knowest not what a day may bring forth." How foolish are those men who wish to pry into futurity! The telescope is ready, and they are going to look through it; but they are so anxious to see, that they breathe on the glass with their hot breath, and they dim it, so that they can discern nothing but clouds and darkness. Oh, ye who are always conjuring up black fiends from the deep unknown, and foolishly vexing your minds with fancies, turn your fancies out of doors, and begin to rest on never-failing promises! Promises are better than forebodings. "Trust in the Lord, and do good; so shalt thou dwell in the land, and verily thou shalt be fed."

Thus I have spoken of the changes of this mortal life.

4. And now, to close, let me ask, WHAT IS TO BE THE END OF THIS LIFE?

We read in the second Book of Samuel, chapter fourteen, and verse fourteen, "We must needs die, and are as water spilt on the ground, which cannot be gathered up again." Man is like a great icicle, which the sun of time is continually thawing, and which is soon to be as water spilt upon the ground, which cannot be gathered up again. Who can recall the departed spirit, or inflate the lungs with a new breath of life? Who can put vitality into the heart, and restore the soul from Hades? None. It cannot be gathered up again; the place that once knew it shall know it no more for ever.

But here a sweet thought charms us. This water cannot be lost, but it shall descend into the soil to filter through the Rock of ages, at last to spring up a pure fountain in heaven, cleansed, purified, and made clear as crystal. How terrible if, on the other hand, it should percolate through the black earth of sin, and hang in horrid drops in the dark caverns of destruction!

Such is life! Then, make the best use of it, my friends, because it is fleeting. Look for another life, because this life is not a very desirable one, it is so changeable. Trust your life in God's hand, because you cannot control its movements; rest in his arms, and rely on his might; for he is able to do for you exceeding abundantly above all that you ask or think; and unto his name be glory for ever and ever! Amen.

A Mother's Death

ALBERT BARNES

I bowed down heavily, as one that mourneth for his mother. — PSALM 35:14.

IN the text it is supposed that the death of a mother affects those who are bereaved by her loss in a peculiar manner, and that such a loss is among the heaviest of sorrows. "I bowed down heavily, as one that mourneth for his mother." To see the force of this text it is not necessary to suppose that this is the heaviest of all sorrows which we can experience, nor is it necessary to make any comparison between this and the other forms of bereavement which we may be called to endure. All that is necessary to say is, that there are chords of the soul touched then which have not been touched before, and which will not be again. A man has but one mother to love; and when such an event occurs it is well for him to endeavor to learn the lessons which God once in his life designs to teach him.

There are usually enough who have been recently afflicted in this manner to make such a topic of public discourse proper. Besides, how large a portion in a congregation is there who have at some time been thus bereaved! How many are there today who at some period of their lives have known what it was to lose a mother! It will be no injury to recall the memory of that scene — not for the purpose of opening wounds again which time and religion may have healed — but to make more fresh in the recollection the lessons which God designed to convey by the living virtues, and by the death of a mother. It may be useful, too, to those who have mothers from whom they may soon be called to part, to contemplate this relation, and to be told of the kind of emotions which spring up in the soul when a parent is taken away to be seen no more. It may teach you to prize their counsels and their friendship more; it may make you more careful not to pain their hearts by unkindness or disobedience.

I shall make no comparison between this relation and that of a father. *That* is in many respects as important and as influential as this; and when that is sundered, the bereavement as much demands the tribute of our tears, and conveys as important lessons to the soul. But though this may be so, the remarks which I propose to submit to you now, will, I trust, be seen to be founded in truth. I shall submit to you a few reflections on such a relation, and such a loss, which I trust may be fitted to be useful.

1. I need hardly say that *the relation of a mother is a peculiar relation, and has features which are found in no other.* The tie is one which exists nowhere else; which can never be renewed; which, when it is sundered, is sundered forever, unless it is cemented by religion, and grows up into eternal affection in the heavens.

Her affection for us was laid far back in her nature, by a benignant Providence, to anticipate our helplessness and our wants as we came into the world. It existed in her heart whatever we were to be, or whatever was to be our fortune in this world, and was so strong that even could she have foreseen all our ingratitude, and all that we might yet do to pain her, she would still have loved us. She met us as we entered on life already prepared to do us good. Her first emotion toward us was that of love; and even then, when we had no character, and no claim for services rendered; when we had furnished no evidence that we ever would be worthy of her love, or repay her kindness with anything but ingratitude, she was ready to do for us what we may even now scarcely secure a friend to do by all our virtues. Not a friend have we now who would watch more patiently by our sick-bed than she would have done by our cradle then, nor have we one who would sorrow more sincerely over our grave. This care we owed primarily to God, and under Him to that affection which He had created in her heart.

> "Unnumbered comforts on my soul,
>   Thy tender care bestowed,
> Before my infant heart conceived
>   From whom those comforts flowed."

The affection thus laid in her heart to anticipate our necessities was strengthened on her part by all her own toil, and care, and watchfulness, and sacrifices on our behalf. Whatever might be the effect on us, the effect on her was to make her love us more. Her own solicitude and toil became thus a measure of her augmented affection; for God has instructed us to love much that which is the fruit of sacrifice and toil. Her love for us was measured far more by her own sacrifices than by our own worth. On our part the attachment formed is not that which grows out of favors rendered, but favors received. It is laid indeed in

nature; but it grows up and expands because we learn more and
more, as we advance in years, how much we owe to a mother.

The attachment for a mother is different from that which we
have for a brother or sister. That may be exceedingly tender
and pure. But it is formed in a different way. When the tie
which binds us to her is severed, it indeed makes a sad desolation in the soul; but it is not precisely the sorrow which we have
when we "bow down heavily, mourning for a mother." We love
a brother or sister, for we began life together. We played together in childhood; we shared the same gentle father to counsel and guide us; and had the same mother to teach us to pray,
and to give us the parting kiss at night. We grew up equally
beloved by our parents, and we have learned to love each other
much by mutual acts of affection and kindness.

The attachment is different from those friendships which we
form as we advance in life. A man leaves father and mother and
cleaves to his wife with an affection more tender and strong than
that formed by any natural relation, but it is not the same. He
forms strong friendships in life, like that which bound the heart
of David and Jonathan, but such friendships did not begin as
we entered on life, nor imbed themselves in the soft heart of infancy and childhood, nor are they cemented by so many acts of
kindness.

The attachment to a mother is different from that which we
form for our children. We love them much — even as she did
us. But it is a love for them as our children; as dependent on
us; as helpless; as needing our care and counsel; as part of ourselves; as those who we hope will do us honor when we are dead.

These attachments which we form in after life, of nature and
affection, are strong and tender; they may be more immediately
tender than those which we bear for a parent; grief may be more
poignant when they are sundered by death, and when we follow
wife or child to the grave, but it has its own features, distinct
from that when a venerable and much loved parent is conveyed
to the tomb. As there was a peculiarity of attachment, so there
will be a peculiarity of sorrow such as we are not to experience
again.

2. *A second peculiarity of feature in this kind of bereavement
is in the change which is produced in our ideas of home — the
home of our childhood and youth.* When she lived there, there
was always a home — a place which in every situation of life we
felt was such, and which we regarded as such.

In our childhood and youth there was in that home where she was, one who always cared for us, and for all that appertained to us. There was one who we were sure would take an interest in everything that we took an interest in, and whose ear we were certain would open to listen to all our tales of childish success or of childish trouble. We were sure that she would take the same interest in it which we did, and we expected confidently that whoever might be against us, she would be for us. We never had a doubt that she would listen to our tale of fright, of disappointment, of calamity; nor that she would feel just as we did about it. The matter might be in itself important or unimportant; it might be dignified or undignified, yet we never doubted that she would regard it as important, and as sufficiently momentous to claim her attention. We had our difficulties in our little world of childhood, but we were sure that there was one who would sympathize with us, and who would be on our side. Our playmates derided us, and laughed at us because we said, in our simplicity, that we would "tell mother." And yet it was philosophy deep and pure to do so — like the pure crystal spring that breaks out of the side of a hill in the uncultivated forest. It was what nature prompted — for nature designed that she should know our troubles, and nature had formed for us such a friend there, that, whoever was against us, we might know she would be on our side; whoever wronged us, she would not; whoever exulted over us, she would not join in the exultation. You may say that this is childish philosophy. So it may be; and the nearer our philosophy comes back to simple nature as developed there, the nearer we shall be to truth. In our troubles we have always needed a friend who would sympathize with us, and to whom we might unburden all the sorrows of the soul. The disciples of John's Redeemer came, and took up his murdered body, "and buried it and went and told Jesus" (Matt. 14:12). In Him they had a friend — tender and delicate above all a mother's feelings — who they were sure would sympathize with their sorrows; and what was more natural than that they should go and tell Him? So in the home of our childhood, it was dear to us as a home, for there was not a sorrow of our heart that we might not tell our mother.

Many of us — most of us who are advanced beyond the period of childhood — went out from that home to embark on the stormy sea of life. Of the feeling of a father, and of his interest in our welfare, we have never entertained a doubt, and our home was

dear because he was there; but there was a peculiarity in the
feeling that it was the home of our mother. While she lived
there, there was a place where we would always be welcome;
one place where we would be met with a smile; one place where
we would be sure of a friend. The world might be indifferent
to us. We might be unsuccessful in our studies or our business.
The new friends which we supposed we had made, might prove
to be false. The honor which we thought we deserved,
might be withheld from us. We might be chagrined and morti-
fied by seeing a rival outstrip us, and bear away the prize which
we sought; but there was a place where no feelings of rivalry
were found, and where those whom the world overlooked would
be sure of a friendly greeting. Whether pale and wan by study,
care, or sickness, or flushed with health and flattering success,
we were sure that we should be welcome there. Amid the storms
that beat upon us and the disappointment that we met with, and
the coldness of the world, we felt still that there was one there
who sympathized in our troubles as well as rejoiced in our success, and that, whatever might be abroad, when we entered the
door of her dwelling, we should be met with a smile. We expected that a mother like the mother of Sisera, as she "looked
out at her window" waiting for the coming of her son laden with
the spoils of victory, would look out for our coming, and that
our return would renew her joy and ours in our earlier days.

> "Oh! in our sterner manhood, when no ray
> Of earlier sunshine glimmers on our way;
> When girt with sin, and sorrow, and the toil
> Of cares, which tear the bosom that they soil;
> Oh! if there be in retrospection's chain
> One link that knits us with young dreams again,
> One thought so sweet, we scarcely dare to muse
> On all the hoarded raptures it reviews,
> Which seems each instant, in its backward range,
> The heart to soften, and its ties to change,
> And every spring untouched for years, to move,
> It is — *the memory of a mother's love!*"

It makes a sad desolation when from such a place a mother
is taken away — and when, whatever may be the sorrows or the
successes in life, she is to greet the returning son or daughter no
more. The home of our childhood may be still lovely. The old
family mansion; the green fields; the running stream; the moss-
covered well; the trees; the lawn; the rose; the sweet-brier, may
be there. Perchance, too, there may be an aged father, with ven-

erable locks, sitting in his loneliness, with everything to com-
mand respect and love. There may be others whom we much
love, but *she* is not there. Her familiar voice is not heard. The
mother has been borne forth to sleep by the side of her children
who went before her, and the place is not what it was.

We may have formed new relations in life — tender and strong
as they can be; we may have another home dear to us as was the
home of our childhood, where there is all in affection, kindness,
and religion to make us happy; but even that home is not what it
was, and it will never be what it was again. There is a loosening
of one of the cords which bound us to earth — designed to prepare us for our eternal flight from everything dear here below,
and to teach us that there is no place here that is to be our permanent home.

3. *A third thing in such an event which is found to convey a
lesson to the soul such as we always feel in bereavement, but
which, like the other things adverted to, has a peculiarity of its
own, is the quickened recollection of our neglects, of our acts of
unkindness, of our ingratitude, of our improper feelings in our
intercourse with those whom we have lost.* What I now advert
to is one of the most beautiful and benignant laws of our nature
— one of the most delicate arrangements to bring our guilt to
remembrance in order that we may exercise true repentance, and
to prompt us to kindness and fidelity in the remaining relations
of life.

This law of our nature, which cannot well be explained except on the supposition that there is a moral government, and
that God designs that all our sins shall be brought to our remembrance, is this — that in the death of a friend we instinctively
recall the wrongs that we may have done him; for some mysterious power seems to summon them up from the land of forgetfulness, and to cause them to pass in solemn procession before us.
Things which we had forgotten; words which we long since uttered but which had passed from the memory; expressions of
irritated feeling; unjust suspicions; jealousies; neglect of the
respect or the courtesies due in that relation of life; a want of
attention when the heart of the friend was sad; want of sympathy in his successes or reverses — all seem to revive as we
stand around the open grave, and as the coffin of the friend descends there.

I said that this was a beautiful and benignant law of our nature, and though attended like other laws when violated, with

pain, the design is as apparent as it is beautiful. It has two objects as a part of the divine moral administration. One is to lead us to repentance for our errors and faults, that we may obtain pardon of our God before it be too late. True, the sleeper there cannot now utter the word of forgiveness. Those lips are forever sealed in death — and how much would we give now could we ask that friend to forgive us! How much would we rejoice could we have the assurance from those lips that the faults that now come thronging on our memory were forgiven and forgotten, and that they did not add a pang to his last sorrows! But if we cannot now confess the fault in the ear of that friend; if we cannot now hope that those lips will open to declare us forgiven, we may confess the fault to God, and may be assured that He will blot the remembrance of it from His book. Around each grave of a friend, therefore, He summons up groups of our past offences that we may be humbled and penitent, and may not go unpardoned to eternity.

The other design of this benignant law is, to keep us from offending hereafter; to teach us to manifest kindness in the remaining relations of life. True, we cannot again injure, or offend, or pain the sleeper there. But there are other hearts that may be made to bleed by ingratitude, or coldness, or neglect, or mercy, and we may be assured that what has happened in the case of the friend that we have now lost, will happen also in theirs. The design of the law is, to teach us to indulge no thought, to speak no word, to evince no feeling which we would regret when they too are removed. And what a restraint would this be on our temper, our words, our whole deportment!

In each bereavement there is a peculiar group of these painful thoughts that come thronging to the recollection. But the occasion requires me only to allude to that class of emotions which is thus summoned to our recollection on the death of a mother. And who is there of us that can see a mother die without many such painful and disquieting thoughts — greatly embittering the natural grief of parting? Even while we were conscious of having had for her strong and tender love; even when in the main we desired to respect her and to make her happy; even when we knew that our general character has been approved by her, and that in life thus far we had not disappointed her fond anticipations, yet how many times in childhood have we been disobedient, how often have we spoken disrespectfully, how often have we disregarded her wishes, how often have we uttered sentiments peevishly that we knew differed from hers; how often have we failed in rendering that prompt and ready obedience which was due to her as a mother, and to her kindness to us; how many times by our perverseness, our self-will, our pride, our obstinacy, have we discouraged her in her efforts to do us good; how often have we done that which would weary out the patience of any one but a parent — and God. Could we hear her speak again, how many things are there which we would wish to confess, and which we would desire her to forgive!

There are many lessons flowing from this subject adapted to those who have but recently been called to this trial — lessons requiring us to submit to God; to be grateful for the example, and counsels, and toils in our behalf of those who have been removed; to imitate them as they imitated their Savior, and to be prepared to follow them to the world of glory. But on these I will not dwell. There are two thoughts, however, which I will suggest.

1. The first relates to those who have had pious mothers, who are now removed to heaven, but whose prayers and counsels they have disregarded. I refer to those who have thus far withheld their hearts from the Savior whom their mother loved, and with whom she now dwells; who have embraced sentiments such as they know she would not approve; who have made choice of companions such as she lived to warn them against; or who indulge in scenes of revelry and sin such as, if she were living, you know would break her heart. Go, young man, and walk in the stillness of the evening among the graves. Beneath your feet, in the sacred slumbers of a Christian death, lies a much-loved mother. How calm her slumbers! How sweet the spot! How lovely a mother's grave! How the memory delights to go back to the nursery, the fireside, the sick-bed, the anxious care of a mother! How it loves to recall her gentle look, her eye of love, her kiss at night! At that grave, thoughtless young man, think of thy revels, thy neglect of God, thy forgetfulness of the prayer that she taught thee, thy friendship now for those against whom she warned thee! She sleeps now in death; but from that grave is it fancy that we hear a voice: "My beloved son! Is this the life that I taught thee to lead? Are these the pleasures which I taught thee to pursue? Did I bear thee, and toil for thee, and wear out my life, that I might train thee for sin, and **death, and hell?"**

2. The other thought relates to those who now have a Christian mother — and who yet disregard her living counsels and prayers. I have adverted to a law of our being, beautiful in its nature, but painful in its inflictions. The day is coming when that mother will die. You may see her die; or far away, you may hear of her death, and may return and visit her grave. Be thou sure that every unkind look, every disobedient action, every harsh word, will come back and visit thy soul. Be sure you will remember everything that ever gave pain to her heart, and remember it with unavailing regret when too late to recall it, or to ask forgiveness. Be sure if you are unkind and disobedient; if you are an infidel or a scoffer; if you slight her counsels and neglect the God and Savior to whom she would conduct you, there are laid up in the chambers of your soul the sources of bitter repentance hereafter — and that you cannot find forgiveness of her whose heart you broke, though you seek it carefully with tears. And be sure that the sweetest of all consolations when she dies, will be found when it is said she has gone to Heaven; and in evidence in your own heart that you will be prepared when the summons comes, to rejoin her in the realms of bliss.

> Into the eternal shadow that girds our life around,
> Into the infinite silence wherewith Death's shore is bound,
> Thou has gone forth, beloved! and I were mean to weep
> That thou has left life's shallows, and dost possess the deep.
>   —Lowell.

Excessive Grief at the Death of Friends

Saint Chrysostom

But I would not have you to be ignorant, brethren, concerning them which are asleep, that ye sorrow not.
— I Thess. 4:13.

WE have occupied four days in explaining to you the parable of Lazarus, to bring out the treasure that we found in a body covered with sores; a treasure, not of gold and silver and precious stones, but of wisdom and fortitude, of patience and endurance. For as in regard to visible treasures, while the surface of the ground shows only thorns and briars, and rough earth, yet, let a person dig deep, abundant wealth discovers itself; so it has proved in respect to Lazarus. Outwardly, wounds; but underneath these, unspeakable wealth; a body pined away, but a noble and wakeful spirit. We have also seen an illustration of that remark of the apostle's — as much as the outward man perishes, so much the inward man is renewed.

It would, indeed, be proper to address you today, also, on this same parable. But to avoid satiety, let us direct the discourse to another subject; for a table with only one sort of food produces satiety, while variety provokes the appetite. That it may be so in regard to our preaching, let us now turn to the blessed Paul. And the things which are to be spoken are harmonious with those that have lately been presented. Hear, then, Paul this day proclaiming — I would not have you be ignorant concerning them which are asleep, that ye sorrow not even as others which have no hope. The parable of Lazarus is the evangelical chord; this passage is the apostolic note. And there is concord between them; for we have, on that parable, said much concerning the resurrection and the future judgment and our discourse now recurs to that theme; so that, though it is on apostolic ground that we are now toiling, we shall here find the same treasure. For in treating the parable, our aim was to teach the hearers this lesson, that they should regard all the splendors of the present life as nothing, but should look forward in their hopes, and daily reflect on the decisions which will be hereafter pronounced, and on that fearful judgment, and that Judge who can not be deceived. On these things Paul has counseled us today in the passages which have been read to us. Attend, however, to his own words — "I would not have you to be ignorant, brethren, concerning them which are asleep, that ye sorrow not, even as others which have no hope. For if we believe that Jesus died and rose again, even so them also which sleep in Jesus will God bring with him."

Say not, a dead man hears not, nor speaks, nor sees, nor is conscious. It is just so with a sleeping person. If I may speak somewhat paradoxically, even the soul of a sleeping person is in some sort asleep; but not so the soul of a dead man; that is awake.

But you say, a dead man experiences corruption, and becomes dust and ashes. And what then, beloved hearers? For this very reason we ought to rejoice. For when a man is about to rebuild an old and tottering house, he first sends out its occupants, then tears it down and rebuilds anew a more splendid one. This occasions no grief to the occupants, but rather joy; for they do not think of the demolition which they see, but of the house which is to come, though not yet seen. When God is about to do a similar work, he destroys our body, and removes the soul which was dwelling in it as from some house, that he may build it anew and more splendidly, and again bring the soul into it with greater glory. Let us not, therefore, regard the tearing down, but the splendor which is to succeed.

If, again, a man has a statue decayed by rust and age, and mutilated in many of its parts, he breaks it up and casts it into a furnace, and after the melting he receives it again in a more beautiful form. As then the dissolving in the furnace was not a destruction but a renewing of the statue, so the death of our bodies is not a destruction but a renovation. When, therefore, you see as in a furnace our flesh flowing away to corruption, dwell not on that sight, but wait for the recasting. And be not satisfied with the extent of this illustration, but advance in your thoughts to a still higher point; for the statuary, casting into the furnace a brazen image, does not furnish you in its place a golden and undecaying statue, but again makes a brazen one. God does not thus; but casting in a mortal body formed of clay, he returns to you a golden and immortal statue; for the earth, receiving a corruptible and decaying body, gives back the same, incorruptible and undecaying. Look not, therefore, on the corpse, **lying with closed eyes and speechless lips, but on the man that** is risen, that has received glory unspeakable and amazing, and direct your thoughts from the present sight to the future hope.

And how is it possible, you ask, not to grieve, since I am only a man? Nor do I say that you should not grieve: I do not condemn dejection, but the intensity of it. To be dejected is natural; but to be overcome by dejection is madness, and folly, and unmanly weakness. You may grieve and weep; but give not way to despondency, nor indulge in complaints. Give thanks to God, who has taken your friend, that you have the opportunity of honoring the departed one, and of dismissing him with becoming funeral rites. If you sink under depression, you withhold honor from the departed, you displease God who has taken him and you injure yourself; but if you are grateful, you pay respect to him, you glorify God, and you benefit yourself. Weep, as wept your master over Lazarus, observing the just limits of sorrow, which it is not proper to pass. Thus also said Paul — "I would not have you to be ignorant concerning them which are asleep, that ye sorrow not as others who have no hope." Grieve, says he; but not as the Greek, who has no hope of a resurrection, who despairs of a future life.

For on what account, tell me, do you thus weep for one departed? Because he was a bad man? You ought on that very account to be thankful, since the occasions of wickedness are now cut off. Because he was good and kind? If so, you ought to rejoice; since he has been soon removed, before wickedness had corrupted him, and he has gone away to a world where he stands ever secure, and there is no room even to mistrust a change. Because he was a youth? For that, too, praise Him that has taken him, because He has speedily called him to a better lot. Because he was an aged man? On this account, also, give thanks and glorify Him that has taken him. Be ashamed of your manner of burial. The singing of psalms, the prayers, the assembling of the (spiritual) fathers and brethren — all this is not that you may weep, and lament, and afflict yourselves, but that you may render thanks to Him who has taken the departed. For as when men are called to some high office, multitudes with praises on their lips assemble to escort them at their departure to their stations, so do all with abundant praise join to send forward, as to greater honor, those of the pious who have departed. Death is rest, a deliverance from the exhausting labors and cares of this world. When, then, thou seest a relative departing, yield not to despondency; give thyself to reflection; examine thy conscience; cherish the thought that after a little while this end awaits thee also. Be more considerate; let another's death excite thee to salutary fear; shake off all indolence; examine your past deeds; quit your sins, and commence a happy change.

Consider to whom the departed has gone, and take comfort. He has gone where Paul is, and Peter, and the whole company of the saints. Consider how he shall arise, with what glory and splendor. Consider, that by mourning and lamenting thou canst not alter the event which has occurred, and that thou wilt in the end injure thyself. Consider whom you imitate by so doing, and shun this companionship in sin. For whom do you imitate and emulate? The unbelieving, those who have no hope; as Paul said — "That ye sorrow not, even as others who have no hope." And observe how carefully he expresses himself; for he does not say, Those who have not the hope of a resurrection, but simply, "Those who have no hope." He that has no hope of a future retribution has no hope at all, nor does he know that there is a God, nor that God exercises a providential care over present occurrences, nor that divine justice looks on all things.

I have now addressed you on this subject, though no one is in particular affliction, that when we shall fall into any such calamity, we may, from the remembrance of what has been said, obtain requisite consolation. As soldiers, even in peace, perform warlike exercises, so that when actually called to battle and the occasion makes a demand for skill, they may avail themselves of the art which they have cultivated in peace; so let us, in time of peace, furnish ourselves with weapons and remedies, that whenever there shall burst on us a war of unreasonable passions, or grief, or pain, or any such thing, we may, well armed and secure on all sides, repel the assaults of the evil one with all skill, and wall ourselves round with right contemplations, with the declarations of God, with the examples of good men, and with every possible defense. For so shall we be able to pass the present life with happiness, and to attain to the kingdom of heaven, through Jesus Christ, to whom be glory and dominion, together with the Father and the Holy Spirit, forever and ever. Amen.

Victory Over Death and the Grave

GEORGE W. BETHUNE

O Death, where is thy sting? O Grave, where is thy victory? The sting of death is sin; and the strength of sin is the law; but thanks be to God, which giveth us the victory through our Lord Jesus Christ.
— I Cor. 15:55-57.

THE sublimity of the text overpowers us. It is the exultation of an inspired apostle. How shall we, weak and imperfect Christians, dare to take words of such fearless joy upon our sinful lips?

My brethren, the apostle, inspired of God, speaks also as a sinner saved by grace. The truth which gives him all his courage, he preaches for our confidence. His conquering Champion, in the fight with death and the grave, "was delivered for our offenses, and was raised again for our justification." He exults as a Christian in God the Savior, and he invites all who receive the gospel to join in his triumphant faith, when he exclaims,

"Thanks be to God, which giveth us the victory through our Lord Jesus Christ!"

It is, therefore, our privilege and our duty to make the words of the text our own. God strengthen us, by their holy teachings, to rejoice in the victory, and to utter the thanksgiving with our whole hearts!

The apostle has demonstrated the glorious resurrection of the just in Christ, by an elaborate argument, and states his conclusion as the fulfillment of Isaiah's prophecy (25:8), that the Lord " will swallow up death in victory, and will wipe away tears from off all faces." "So," say he (vs. 54), "when this corruptible shall have put on incorruption, and this mortal shall have put on immortality, then shall be brought to pass this saying that is written: 'Death is swallowed up in victory.' " His pious soul, with that faith "which is the substance of things hoped for," anticipates the full triumph, now made certain by the resurrection and ascension to glory of Christ the Savior, the Life and Forerunner of his church. He remembers the prom-

34

ise of God by the prophet Hosea (13:14): "I will ransom them from the power of the grave; I will redeem them from death: O death, I will be thy plagues; O grave, I will be thy destruction"; and in a burst of eloquent exultation, he defies his former enemies: "O death, where is thy sting! O grave, where is thy victory!" Thou hadst a sting, O death! "The sting of death is sin"; and that sting was deadly. "The strength of sin is the law"; but now is thy sting plucked out, and all its venom turned into life. "Thanks be to God, which giveth us the victory, through our Lord Jesus Christ!"

The natural division of the text, and that which we shall follow, is: 1. The Challenge: "O Death, where is thy sting! O Grave, where is thy victory!" 2. The Thanksgiving: "Thanks be to God which giveth us the victory through our Lord Jesus Christ!"

1. The Challenge:

"O Death, where is thy sting! O Grave, where is thy victory!"

The apostle, following Hosea, and by a strong figure, challenges death and the grave separately, though, strictly, they are one. The victory of the grave is the consequence of the sting of death. It is a bold challenge to demand of Death, Where is thy sting? and of the Grave, Where is thy victory?

Where is the sting of death? Alas! and is it nothing to die? Nothing to be made sure that we must die? Is it nothing to leave this fair earth, the light of the cheerful sun, our pleasant homes, our loving friends, and to be buried and become as dust beneath the sod, and under the shade of the gloomy cypresses? Is it nothing to close our senses forever upon all we have cherished, and sought, and hoped for, and prided ourselves in? Is it nothing to have the sad certainty before us at all times, in the midst of our best successes, that the hour is coming when the cold, narrow, ignominious grave, shall hide us from them all? That our plans, contrive them and pursue them as we may, of ambition, gain, knowledge, service to those who are dear, zeal for our country and the welfare of mankind, must be broken off, and the brain which projected, the hand which wrought, and the heart which beat strong, become still as the clod, and the luxury of worms? Is it nothing that every step of humanity, the first tottering effort of the crowing child, the sportive spring of youth, the firm tread of adult vigor, and the halt of the old man, leaning upon his staff, is to the same vile end? That every hour of sleep or activity, pleasure or sorrow, thoughtfulness or gaiety,

alike urges us irresistibly on? Is it nothing that the blood shall
be chilled at its fountain, and the clammy sweat-drops start out
upon the forehead, and the breath come slow, and in agony, and
the life, clinging desperately, be torn away and cast forth by
fierce convulsion?

Has death no sting, when we hold the beloved, who made life
precious and the world beautiful, by so frail, brief, melancholy a
tenure? Has it no sting for the yearning bosom, from whose
warm sanctuary the little one has been taken, never again to
nestle sweetly there at waking morn, or for the noon-tide sleep,
or in the drowsy evening?

Has it no sting in that "life-long pang a widowed spirit bears?"
Has it no sting when the faces, which reflected our smiles, and
beamed back upon us tenderness, and sympathy, and faith, are
so changed that we must send them away and bury them out of
our sight? Or when we follow the good man, the just, the gen-
erous, the friend of the sorrowful and the stranger and the poor,
the wise teacher of truth, the advocate of right, and the champion of the weak, to that bourne from which he will return to
bless the world no more? No sting in death? Is there one among
us such a miracle of uninterrupted happiness, so insensible to
others' grief, as not to have felt its keen and lingering sharpness?

Where is the victory of the grave? Where is it not? Power
can not resist it. The kings of the earth lie in "the desolate
places they built for themselves." Riches can purchase no allies
skillful to avert the blow. The marble in its sculptured pomp
acknowledges the struggle to have been in vain. There is no discharge in this war for wisdom, or youth, or virtue, or strength.
In the crowded burial-place they lie together, smitten down by
the same hand. Obscurity affords us refuge. The slave falls beside his master, and the beggar is slain by the wayside. Some
may maintain the fight a little longer, but "the same event hap-
peneth unto all."

Where is the victory of the grave? What conqueror is so
mighty, when all conquerors fight in its battles, and then bow
themselves to death with their victims? The track of its march
is cumbered with the wreck of fairest symmetry, and beauty, and
vigor. The entire generations of past ages are crumbled into
dust; all the living are following in one vast funeral; all pos-
terity shall follow us. Were all the cries of those who have per-
ished by flood, or battle, or famine, or fire, or sickness, and the
wails of the bereaved over their dead, crowded into one, the

shriek would shake the earth to the center. Were all the corpses that are crumbling or have crumbled to dust, laid upon the surface, as the slain upon a battlefield, there would not be room for the living among the disfigured trophies of the conquering grave, which, with the world for its prison-house, must consume its captives to make room for more. Where is the victory of the grave? The silence of the dead, the anguish of the surviving, the mortality of all that shall be born of mortals, confess it to be universal.

Yet, were there nothing beside this, the calamity would be light. A gloomy anticipation, a few tears, a sharp pang, and all would be over. We should sleep, and dream not. We should forget, and be forgotten. But there is more than this. Whence came death? Why must man, with his upward-bearing countenance, his vast affections, his far-reaching thought, the most fearfully made of all God's wonderful works, die? How came there to be graves in this decorated earth, which God looked down upon with smiles, and pronounced very good? My fellow-children of the dust, God is angry with us. None but God could take the life God gave, or dissolve what God has made. God has armed Death with fatal strength, and sent him forth, the executioner of a divine sentence, the avenger of a broken law. The victory of the grave is the conquest of justice over rebellion. It is omnipotence, putting to shame and eternal defeat the treason of man against his Maker. It is holiness consuming the sinner. Death is God's wrath, for his favor is life.

"The sting of death is sin, and the strength of sin is the law." Death had no sting for man, and the grave no victory, till sin entered into the world; but now "death hath passed upon all men, for that all have sinned." The law of God, which condemns the sinner, gives Death power to seize and hold him fast, with all the strength of God's wrath against the guilty. Wherever there is sin, its wages are death. Wherever death is, there must be sin. Yes! even in thy death, thou sinless, crucified Lamb of God, for thou didst bear the sins of thy people! It is enough that we are mortal, to prove that we are sinners, and condemned already by him who declares, "the soul that sinneth it shall die." Does any one doubt this? Let him solve the question why God slays his creatures. There is no evading it. Man must be a sinner, or his Maker a tyrant.

Here is the sharpness of death's sting. It is the evidence and punishment of sin. It is the lowering darkness of the storm of wrath, which is eternal. It is the hand of God tearing the sinner's shrieking spirit out of the world, and dragging him to judgment, thence to be cast down into pangs everlasting; while the grave holds the body in its unyielding grasp, till the Son of man comes in the clouds to execute his final vengeance upon each guilty soul, and its guilty instrument the polluted flesh. O my hearers, it is the bitterness of death, that pleasant as sins may be now, death will soon and surely come; and after death the judgment, when every sin shall find us out, and the sinner have no excuse, nor plea, nor refuge from the flashing terrors of the inexorable law; and after the judgment, eternal woe for all the condemned, and a prison-house, whose doors allow no escape, where remorse preys upon the soul like a venemous worm that never dies, and the wrath of God burns in fire unquenchable. O my God, what a strange lethargy must that sinner be in, who feels not the sting of death, but sleeps stupidly on, dreaming of lust, and gain, and pride, till death wakens him with eternal agony!

Here we see the apostle's boldness, the strength and valor of Christian faith; for, knowing that he must die, and the grave cover him, he stands up bravely, and flings defiance in their faces:

"O Death, where is thy sting? O Grave, where is thy victory?"

To learn the secret of his courage, we must consider,

2. The Thanksgiving.

"Thanks be to God, which giveth us the victory through our Lord Jesus Christ!"

This with the preceding verse, answers three questions: Whence is the victory? How is it given us? In what does it consist?

1. *"Thanks be to God, which giveth us the victory!"*

God gives death its sting, and the grave its victory. So long as God arms and strengthens them, it is impossible to resist them. They are God's ministers, and in their ministry omnipotent. God, therefore, alone can give us the victory, by becoming our friend. When he is our friend, his ministers, which were our enemies, must be our friends and servants. Thus the believer looks to God, and relies wholly upon him. If there be no help from God, there can be none. He hopes not to deserve, or earn, or work the victory for himself. It must be given him by an act of free grace, sovereign mercy, and redeeming love. But when God comes to his rescue, his deliverance is certain. Therefore he says, "thanks be to God!"

2. *How is the victory given?* Will the sting remain with death? or strength with the grave? If so, how will the believer conquer? Will God arm his enemies against him, and yet fight for him? Will omnipotence contend with omnipotence? or mercy deliver the sinner whom justice holds bound? Does sin cease to be guilty, or the law abate its force? Hear the apostle.

"Thanks be to God, which giveth us the victory *through our Lord Jesus Christ.*"

"The sting of death is sin, and the strength of sin is the law." Death is the penalty of sin, and, while the law condemns the sinner, he must remain captive to death and the grave. But our Lord Jesus Christ, by satisfying the law for his people, plucked out the sting of death, and ravished the victory from the grave.

For this the Son of God became incarnate, that, as man, in the place of man the sinner, he might be capable of suffering the punishment of the law, which is death; while his indwelling divinity gave to those sufferings an infinite worth. As God, he had the power to dissolve the bonds of death; but as the Redeemer, by his infinite atonement, he purchased the right to remit the penalty of the law, which passed death upon the sinner. He became man to suffer; he died that man might live. This the apostle expressly says (Heb. 2:9), that Jesus "was made a little" (or, as some read, a little while) "lower than the angels for the suffering of death"; and, again (14, 15), "Forasmuch, then, as the children are partakers of flesh and blood, he also himself took part of the same, that through death he might destroy him that had the power of death; that is, the devil (the tormentor of the damned sinner), and deliver them, who through fear of death, were all their life-time subject to bondage."

He stood forth in our stead, to answer all the demands of the law against us; and the Sovereign Lawgiver accepted the substitute, and laid upon him the iniquity of us all. Then, having for us honored the law, by a life of perfect obedience, and infinite merit, he came to the passion of death. On the cross he invoked the death we deserved, in its most cruel and shameful forms. He stood between the venomed monster and us, and into his heart death struck his sting deep, so deep that he could not draw it forth again; and losing all his power to harm, hung gasping and dying with the dying Savior, and died in slaying Christ. In plain words, he exhausted the penalty, and satisfied the law, and thus death lost all its strength to hurt those who by faith are crucified with Christ.

More than this, he demonstrated his victory over the grave. For, though he was buried, and the stone rolled to the door of the sepulcher in the rock, and sealed and guarded, and the grave and the powers of darkness struggled mightily to hold him fast, "it was not possible that he could be holden by them"; but, bursting the bars asunder, he dragged them forth, captivity captive, making an ostentation of his spoils, openly triumphing. Thus did God the Father own him as his Son, and acknowledge the penalty paid, the atonement complete. Thus did the Holy Spirit crown him conqueror, and anoint him Prince of Life. Thus did he show himself to the believing sight of his church, as their triumphant champion, JEHOVAH THEIR RIGHTEOUSNESS, and their "Living Way" through death and the grave, to the glory on high.

But the full manifestation of his triumph and ours, is kept for that day when the voice of the archangel and the trump of God shall proclaim his final coming to judgment; and all the dead, the countless dead, whose dust is scattered over the earth, beneath the sea, and in the very air, shall start to life; his redeemed, glorious in beauty, incorruptible, like his own glorified body, to shine with him, his brightest trophies, forever; and the wicked, who would not have him to reign over them, confounded and terrified by the terrible splendor of the once crucified Jesus, to hear the sentence of death, whose mortal agonies are eternal, and to be cast down to shame unspeakable, horror, and fiery torment, whose smoke shall rise forever. Thus will our Lord vindicate his conquest over death and the grave, by compelling them to give freedom to the holy bodies of the redeemed; that, as Adam walked in Paradise, body and soul, a perfect man, they, in their entire humanity, may enter the second Paradise of their inheritance undefiled, and that fadeth not away; and by making them ministers of his just vengeance upon the souls and bodies of all the wicked.

3. *Wherein does our victory, through the Lord Jesus Christ, consist?*

"Thanks be to God, which giveth us the victory through our Lord Jesus Christ!"

The believer triumphs in Christ's perfect atonement.

By faith he is born again with Christ, and as Christ became incarnate for him, so is Christ formed in him, the hope of glory.

By faith he obeys in Christ, walks with Christ in his holy life, and through Christ honors the divine law, which before he had broken. By faith he is crucified with Christ: "I am crucified with Christ," says the apostle (Gal. 2:20). Every drop of the bloody sweat, every pang of the lacerated flesh, every agony of the sinking spirit, in which Christ poured out his soul unto death, went to pay his penalty, and discharge him from the grasp of death, the executioner of the law's vengeance.

For him death has no more sting. Death remains. Its precursors, pain and sickness and infirmity remain. But their mastery over him exists no longer. He knows that they are changed. The curse is changed to blessing, the enemies to friends. Pain and sickness and infirmity are now God's faithful chastenings; not precursors of death, but of a far more exceeding and an eternal weight of glory; and death is no more death, but life, life eternal, life exalted and heavenly.

The grave has no victory over him; for there he buried his sins, his sorrows, his misery, lusts and vileness. He leaves his body there to be purified against the final redemption, while his soul goes free to exult where it can feel no shackle, no warring law, nor foul temptation. Thus he bears affliction with patient hope, as he would take a medicine with the certainty of better health, or submit to surgery, that an inveterate plague may be eradicated; and he calmly awaits the coming of death to unbolt his prison door, knock off his fetters, and lead him forth into purer air and boundless delight. The sting of death lost its power when his sins were pardoned; and death itself waits like a captive upon its Christian master.

The believer triumphs in Christ's resurrection. "I am crucified with Christ, nevertheless I live, yet not I, but Christ liveth in me," says the apostle (Gal. 2:20). He was dead in trespasses and sins; but as the apostle reasons in Ephesians, first and second chapters, he is quickened, together with Christ's body, by the same Holy Spirit, to a new and better life. He has a divine life in him. He is a new man in Christ Jesus; not in body, for there are natural causes which render its dissolution necessary; but a new man in soul, strengthened to bear the burden and resist the evil lusts of the flesh. Eternal life is begun in him, faint, indeed, as life in the new-born babe; but, more than the earnest, the very pulsations of immortality. For this is the office and power of Christ, to give *eternal* life to as many as receive him; and this is the privilege of the Christian, even on earth, to have his conversation in heaven. Death has lost its power to divide him from God. He soars upon the wings of faith far above and beyond the gloomy barrier, enters the company of the church of the first-born, and listens to the harpings of innumerable angels. Is not this a victory over death and the grave?

The believer triumphs in the final resurrection. Christ not only arose, but ascended up on high. There the body, which was here bent by sorrow, has been made glorious in divine beauty; and the countenance, here channeled by tears, buffeted and spit upon, is altogether lovely, the radiation of its smile, the fairest light of heaven; and the crown of all power, might, and dominion, is bright in the splendor of many priceless jewels upon the brow scarred by the mocking thorns; and heaven rolls up its waves of hallelujahs to the feet, in which the prints of the nails perpetuate the memory of the cross; and the hands, yet manifesting the cruel malice of men, are stretched forth to bless the countless throngs uttering praises to the name of Jesus, the Lamb that was slain.

As the Redeemer is glorified in his flesh, so shall the believer be raised up to glory at the last day. What then to him, whose faith can grasp things hoped for and unseen, are all the passing ignominies, and pangs, and insults, which now afflict the follower of the man of sorrows, the Lord of life and glory? Every revolution of the earth rolls on to that fullness of adoption, "when this mortal shall put on immortality, and this corruption shall put on incorruption, and shall be brought to pass this saying, Death is swallowed up in victory"; When these eyes now so dim and soon to be closed in dust, shall behold the face of God in righteousness; when these hands, now so weak and stained with sin, shall bear aloft the triumphant palm, and strike the golden harp that seraphs love to listen to; and these voices, now so harsh and tuneless, shall swell in Trisagion, the thrice holy of the angels. Yes, beloved Master, we see thee, "who wast made a little lower than the angels for the suffering of death, crowned with glory and honor;" and thou hast promised that we shall share thy glory and thy crown!

"Thanks be to God, which giveth us the victory, through our Lord Jesus Christ!" "Us!" And who are included in that sublime and multitudinous plural? "Not to me only," says the apostle, "but to all them that love his appearing" (II Tim. 4:8). Ye shall share it, ancient believers, who, from Adam to Christ, worshiped by figure, and under the shadow! Ye shall share it, ye prophets, who wondered at the mysterious promises of glory following suffering! Ye shall share it, ye mighty apostles, though ye doubted when ye heard of the broken tomb! Ye, martyrs, whose howling enemies execrated you, as they slew you by sword, and cross, and famine, and rack, and the wild beast, and flame! And ye, God's humble poor, whom men despised; but of whom the world was not worthy, God's angels are watching, as they watched the sepulcher in the garden, over your obscure graves, keeping your sacred dust till the morning break, when it shall be crowned with princely splendor! Yes, thou weak one, who yet hast strength to embrace thy Master's cross! Thou sorrowing one, whose tears fall like rain, but not without hope, over the grave of thy beloved! Thou tempted one, who, through much tribulation, art struggling on to the kingdom of God! Ye all shall be there, and ten thousand times ten thousand more! Hark! the trumpet! The earth groans and rocks herself as if in travail! They rise, the sheeted dead; but how lustrously white are their garments! How dazzling their beautiful holiness! What a mighty host! They fill the air; they acclaim hallelujahs; the heavens bend with shouts of harmony; the Lord comes down, and his angels are about him; and he owns his chosen, and they rise to meet him and they mingle with cherubim and seraphim, and the shoutings are like thunders from the throne — thunderings of joy: "Death, where is thy sting! O Grave, where is thy victory! Thanks be to God which giveth us the victory, through our Lord Jesus Christ!"

Christian, death is before us. The graves are thick around us. There lie many dear — dearer because they are dead. We must soon lie with them.

I do not say, Suffer not — Jesus suffered. Faith teaches no stoicism. But suffer like men valiant in battle, whose wounds, when they smart the most, are incentives to new courage, and earnests of future honor.

I do not say, Weep not — Jesus wept. But sorrow not for the Christian dead. They are safe and blest. Weep for the sins that unfit you to follow them.

I do not say, Shudder not at the thought of death — Jesus trembled when he took the cup into his hand, dropping with bloody sweat. It is human nature to shrink from the grave. But I can say, Fear not. Now it is your duty to live. When death comes you shall have grace to die. Look through the dark avenue. Think of the good who are awaiting you at home, in our

Father's house; think of the precious ones for whom you weep; but who weep no more. Fear not to leave behind you the living, whom you have commended to Jesus; he will remember your trust. Be ready to go where you shall not be unwelcome to your Father, your Savior, and the family around the throne. There await the resurrection morning, when the family shall be complete — "no wanderer lost."

But O! be sure that you are in Christ; that you are covered by his atonement; that you have indeed received the spirit of adoption, and have put on the whole armor of God. Then may you be sure of the victory.

But O, my God, what shall I say to those who have no faith in thee, no repentance, no consideration? They are going down to death and the grave; yet they live and laugh on, as though they were to live here forever! How shall I tell them of the sting of death! The victory of the grave! The sting of eternal death! The grave of everlasting fire! Speak thou to them, O Holy Spirit! O merciful Savior! O Father, pitiful of thy children! Turn them, draw them, compel them, to come under the wings of thy pardoning love! Spare them from a hopeless death, an unsanctified grave, judgment without an advocate in Christ, and the bitter pains of body and soul in hell forever!

The Nature of the Saint's Rest

RICHARD BAXTER

There remaineth therefore a rest unto the people of God.
— Heb. 4:9.

IT was not only our interest in God, and actual enjoyment of
him, which was lost in Adam's fall, but all spiritual knowledge of him, and true disposition toward such a felicity. When
the Son of God comes with recovering grace and discoveries of
a spiritual and eternal happiness and glory, he finds not faith in
man to believe it. As the poor man, that would not believe any
one had such a sum as a hundred pounds, so men will hardly
now believe there is such a happiness as Christ hath procured.
When God would give the Israelites his Sabbaths of rest in a
land of rest, it was harder to make them believe it than to overcome their enemies and procure it for them. And when they
had it, only as a small intimation and earnest of an incomparably
more glorious rest through Christ, they yet believe no more
than they possess; or, if they expect more from the Messiah, it
is only the increase of their earthly felicity. The apostle clearly
proves that the end of all ceremonies and shadows is to direct
men to Jesus Christ, the substance; and that the rest of Sabbaths
and Canaan should teach them to look for a further rest, which
indeed is their happiness. My text is his conclusion after divers
arguments; a conclusion which contains the ground of all the believers' comfort, the end of all his duty and sufferings, the life
and sum of all gospel promises and Christian privileges.

What is more welcome to men under personal afflictions, tir-
ing duties, disappointments, or sufferings, than rest? It is not
our comfort only, but our stability. Our liveliness in all duties,
our enduring of tribulation, our honoring of God, the vigor of
our love, thankfulness and all our graces; yea, the very being of
our religion and Christianity depend on the believing, serious
thoughts of our rest. And now, reader, whoever thou art, young
or old, rich or poor, I entreat thee and charge thee, in the name
of thy Lord, who will shortly call thee to a reckoning and judge
thee to thy everlasting, unchangeable state, that thou give not
these things the reading only, and so dismiss them with a bare

approbation; but that thou set upon this work, and take God in Christ for thy only rest, and fix thy heart upon him above all. May the living God, who is the portion and rest of his saints, make these our carnal minds so spiritual, and our earthly hearts so heavenly, that loving him and delighting in him may be the work of our lives; and that neither I that write nor you that read this book may ever be turned from this path of life; "lest, a promise being left us of entering into his rest," we should "come short of it," through our own unbelief or negligence.

The saints' rest is the most happy state of a Christian; or, it is the perfect endless enjoyment of God by the perfected saints, according to the measure of their capacity, to which their souls arrive at death, and both soul and body most fully after the resurrection and final judgment.

I. *There are some things necessarily presupposed in the nature of this rest.*

1. *That mortal men are the persons seeking it.* For angels and glorified spirits have it already, and the devils and damned are past hope.

2. *That they choose God only for their end and happiness.* He that takes any thing else for his happiness is out of the way the first step.

3. *That they are distant from this end.* This is the woeful case of all mankind since the fall. When Christ comes with regenerating grace, he finds no man sitting still, but all hastening to eternal ruin and making haste toward hell; till by conviction he first brings them to a stand, and then by conversion turns their hearts and lives sincerely to himself. This end, and its excellency, is supposed to be known and seriously intended.

And not only a distance from this rest, but the true knowledge of this distance, is also supposed. They that never yet knew they were without God, and in the way to hell, never yet knew the way to heaven. Can a man find that he hath lost his God and his soul, and not cry, I am undone? The reason why so few obtain this rest is they will not be convinced that they are, in point of title, distant from it, and, in point of practice, contrary to it. Who ever sought for that which he knew not he had lost? "They that be whole need not a physician, but they that are sick."

4. *The influence of a superior moving cause is also supposed.* If God move us not, we can not move. It is a most necessary part of our Christian wisdom to keep our subordination to God and dependence on him. "We are not sufficient of ourselves to

think any thing as of ourselves, but our sufficiency is of God."
"Without me," says Christ, "ye can do nothing."

5. *It is next supposed, that they who seek this rest have an
inward principle of spiritual life.* God does not move men like
stone, but he endows them with life, not to enable them to move
without him, but in subordination to himself, the first Mover.

6. *And further, this rest supposes such an actual tendency of
soul toward it as is regular and constant, earnest and laborious.*
He that hides his talent shall receive the wages of a slothful servant. Christ is the door, the only way to this rest. "But strait is
the gate and narrow is the way"; and we must *strive,* if we will
enter. And, he only "that endureth to the end shall be saved."
And never did a soul obtain rest with God whose desire was not
set upon him above all things else in the world. "Where your
treasure is, there will your heart be also." The remainder of
our old nature will much weaken and interrupt these desires,
but never overcome them. And, considering the opposition to
our desires, from the contrary principles in our nature, and from
the weakness of our graces, together with our continued distance from the end, our tendency to that end must be laborious,
and with all our might. All these things are pre-supposed, in
order to a Christian's obtaining an interest in heavenly rest.

II. Now we have ascended these steps into the outward court,
let us look within the veil, and show *what this rest contains.*
Alas! how little know I of that glory! The glimpse which Paul
had, contained what could not, or must not, be uttered. Had he
spoken the things of heaven in the language of heaven, and none
understood that language, what the better? The Lord reveal to
me what I may reveal to you! The Lord open some light, and
show both you and me our inheritance! Not as to Moses, who
had only a discovery instead of possession, and saw the land
which he never entered; but as the pearl was revealed to the mer-
chant in the gospel, who rested not till he had sold all he had
and bought it.

1. *One thing contained in heavenly rest is the ceasing from
means of grace.* When we have obtained the haven, we have
done sailing. When the workman receives his wages it is im-
plied he has done his work. When we are at our journey's end,
we have done with the way. Whether tongues, they shall cease;
whether knowledge, it also, so far as it had the nature of means,
shall vanish away. There shall be no more prayer, because no
more necessity, but the full enjoyment of what we prayed for:

neither shall we need to fast, and weep, and watch any more, being out of the reach of sin and temptations. Preaching is done; the ministry of man ceases; ordinances become useless; the laborers are called in, because the harvest is gathered, the tares burned, and the work finished; the unregenerate past hope, and the saints past fear, for ever.

2. *There is in heavenly rest a perfect freedom from all evils:* from all the evils that accompanied us through our course, and which necessarily follow our absence from the chief good, besides our freedom from those eternal flames and restless miseries which the neglectors of Christ and grace must for ever endure; a woeful inheritance, which, both by birth and actual merit, was due to us as well as to them! In heaven there is nothing that defileth or is unclean. All that remains without. And doubtless there is not such a thing as grief and sorrow known there; nor is there such a thing as a pale face, a languid body, feeble joints, helpless infancy, decrepit age, peccant humors, painful or pining sickness, gripping fears, consuming cares, not whatsoever deserves the name of evil. Our sorrow is turned to joy, and our joy shall no man take from us.

3. *Another ingredient of this rest is, the highest degree of the saints' personal perfection, both of body and soul.* Were the glory ever so great, and themselves not made capable of it by a personal perfection suitable thereto, it would be little to them. "Eye hath not seen, nor ear heard, neither hath entered into the heart of man, the things which God hath prepared for them that love him." For the eye of flesh is not capable of seeing them, nor this ear of hearing them, nor this heart of understanding them: but there, the eye, and ear, and heart are made capable; else, how do they enjoy them? The more perfect the sight is, the more delightful the beautiful object. The more perfect the appetite, the sweeter the food. The more musical the ear, the more pleasant the melody. The more perfect the soul, the more joyous those joys, and the more glorious to us is that glory.

4. *The principal part of this rest is our nearest enjoyment of God, the chief good.* And here, reader, wonder not if I be at a loss, and if my apprehensions receive but little of that which is in my expressions. If it did not appear to the beloved disciple what we shall be, but only, in general, "that when Christ shall appear we shall be like him," no wonder if I know little. When I know so little of God, I can not much know what it is to enjoy him. If I know so little of spirits, how little of the Father of

spirits, or the state of my own soul, when advanced to the enjoyment of him! I stand and look upon a heap of ants, and see
them all at one view: they know not me, my being, nature, or
thoughts, though I am their fellow-creature: how little, then,
must we know of the great Creator, though he, with one view,
clearly beholds us all! A glimpse, the saints behold as in a glass,
which makes us capable of some poor, dark apprehensions of
what we shall behold in glory. If I should tell a worldling what
the holiness and spiritual joys for the saints on earth are, he can
not know; for grace can not be clearly known without grace;
how much less could he conceive it, should I tell him of this
glory! But to the saints I may be somewhat more encouraged
to speak, for grace gives them a dark knowledge and slight taste
of glory.

O the full joys offered to a believer in that one sentence of
Christ, "Father, I will that they whom thou hast given me be
with me where I am, that they may behold my glory which thou
hast given me!" Every word is full of life and joy. If the Queen
of Sheba had cause to say of Solomon's glory, "Happy are thy
men, happy are these thy servants, who stand continually before
thee, and hear thy wisdom"; then, surely they that stand continually before God, and see his glory, and the glory of the Lamb,
are more than happy. To them will Christ give to eat of the tree
of life, and to eat of the hidden manna; yea, he will make them
pillars in the temple of God, and they shall go no more out; and
he will write upon them the name of his God, and the name of
the city of his God, which is New Jerusalem, which cometh down
out of heaven from his God, and he will write upon them his
new name; yea, more, if more may be, he will grant them to sit
with him in his throne. "These are they who came out of great
tribulation, and have washed their robes, and made them white
in the blood of the Lamb; therefore are they before the throne
of God, and serve him day and night in his temple, and he that
sitteth on the throne shall dwell among them. The Lamb, which
is in the midst of the throne, shall feed them, and shall lead them
unto living fountains of water; and God shall wipe away all tears
from their eyes." O blind, deceived world; can you show us
such a glory? This is the city of our God, where the tabernacle
of God is with men, and he will dwell with them, and they shall
be his people, and God himself shall be with them, and be their
God. The glory of God shall lighten it, and the Lamb is the
light thereof. And there shall be no more curse; but the throne

of God and of the Lamb shall be in it; and his servants shall serve him, and they shall see his face, and his name shall be in their foreheads. These sayings are faithful and true, and the things which must shortly be done.

And now we say, as Mephibosheth, let the world take all, forasmuch as our Lord will come in peace. Rejoice, therefore, in the Lord, O ye righteous! and say, with his servant David, "The Lord is the portion of mine inheritance: the lines are fallen unto me in pleasant places; yea, I have a goodly heritage. I have set the Lord always before me; because he is at my right hand, I shall not be moved. Therefore my heart is glad and my glory rejoiceth; my flesh also shall rest in hope. For thou wilt not leave my soul in hell, neither wilt thou suffer thine Holy One to see corruption. Thou wilt show me the path of life; in thy presence is fulness of joy; at thy right hand there are pleasures for evermore."

Be of good cheer, Christian; the time is at hand when God and thou shalt be near, and as near as thou canst well desire. It is better to be "a door-keeper in the house of God, than to dwell in the tents of wickedness." Thou shalt ever stand before him, about his throne, in the room with him, in his presence-chamber. Wouldst thou yet be nearer? Thou shalt be his child, and he thy Father; thou shalt be an heir to his kingdom; yea, more, the spouse of his Son. And what more canst thou desire? Thou shalt be a member of the body of his Son; he shall be thy Head; thou shalt be one with him, who is one with the Father, as he himself hath desired for thee of his Father: "That they all may be one, as thou, Father, art in me, and I in thee, that they also may be one in us; and the glory which thou gavest me, I have given them, that they may be one, even as we are one; I in them, and thou in me, that they may be made perfect in one, and that the world may know that thou hast sent me, and hast loved them as thou has loved me."

5. *We must add, that this rest contains a sweet and constant action of all the powers of the soul and body in this enjoyment of God.* This *body* shall be so changed that it shall no more be flesh and blood, which can not inherit the kingdom of God; but a spiritual body. We sow not that body which shall be, but God giveth it a body as it hath pleased him, and to every seed his own body. If grace makes a Christian differ so much from what he was as to say, I am not the man I was; how much more will glory make us differ! As much as a body spiritual, above the

sun in glory, exceeds these frail, noisome, diseased bodies of flesh, so far shall our senses exceed those we now possess. Doubtless, as God advances our senses and enlarges our capacity, so will he advance the happiness of those senses, and fill up, with himself, all that capacity. Certainly the body would not be raised up and continued, if it were not to share in the glory. As it hath shared in the obedience and sufferings, so shall it also in the blessedness. As Christ bought the whole man, so shall the whole partake of the everlasting benefits of the purchase. O blessed employment of a glorified body! to stand before the throne of God and the Lamb, and to sound forth for ever, "Thou art worthy, O Lord, to receive glory, and honor, and power. Worthy is the Lamb that was slain, to receive power, and riches, and wisdom and strength, and honor, and glory, and blessing; for thou hast redeemed us to God, by thy blood, out of every kindred, and tongue, and people, and nation; and hast made us unto our God kings and priests. Alleluia: salvation, and glory, and honor, and power, unto the Lord our God. Alleluia, for the Lord God omnipotent reigneth." O Christians! this is the blessed rest; a rest, as it were, without rest; for "they rest not day and night, saying, Holy, holy, holy Lord God Almighty, who was, and is, and is to come." And if the body shall be thus employed, O how shall the soul be taken up! As its powers and capacities are greatest, so its actions are strongest, and its enjoyments sweetest. As the bodily senses have their proper actions, whereby they receive and enjoy their objects, so does the soul in its own actions enjoy its own objects by knowing, remembering, loving, and delightful joying. This is the soul's enjoyment. By these eyes it sees, and by these arms it embraces.

Knowledge, of itself, is very desirable. As far as the rational soul exceeds the sensitive, so far the delights of a philosopher, in discovering the secrets of nature and knowing the mystery of sciences, exceed the delights of the drunkard, the voluptuary, or the sensualist. So excellent is all truth. What, then, is their delight who knows the God of truth! How noble a faculty of the soul is the understanding! It can compass the earth; it can measure the sun, moon, stars, and heaven; it can foreknow each eclipse to a minute, many years before. But this is the top of all its excellency, that it can know God, who is infinite, who made all these — a little here, and more, much more, hereafter. O the wisdom and goodness of our blessed Lord! He hath created the understanding with a natural bias and inclination to truth, as its object; and to the prime truth, as its prime object. Christian, when, after long gazing heavenward, thou hast got a glimpse of Christ, dost thou not sometimes seem to have been with Paul in the third heaven, whether in the body or out, and to have seen what is unutterable? Art thou not, with Peter, ready to say, "Master, it is good to be here"? "O that I might dwell in this mount! O that I might ever see what I now see!" Didst thou never look so long upon the Sun of Righteousness till thine eyes were dazzled with his astonishing glory? And did not the splendor of it make all things below seem dark and drear to thee? Especially in the day of suffering for Christ, when he usually appears most manifestly to his people, didst thou never see one walking in the midst of the fiery furnace with thee, like the Son of God? Believe me, Christians, yea, believe God; you that have known most of God in Christ here, it is as nothing to what you shall know: in comparison of that it scarce deserves to be called knowledge. For as these bodies, so that knowledge must cease, that a more perfect may succeed. "Knowledge shall vanish away. For we know in part. But when that which is perfect is come, then that which is in part shall be done away. When I was a child, I spake as a child, I understood as a child, I thought as a child; but, when I became a man, I put away childish things. For now we see through a glass darkly, but then face to face; now I know in part, but then shall I know even as also I am known." Marvel not, therefore, Christian, how it can be life eternal to know God and Jesus Christ. To enjoy God and Christ is eternal life: and the soul's enjoying is in knowing. They that savor only of earth and consult with flesh think it a poor happiness to know God. "But we know that we are of God, and the whole world lieth in wickedness; and we know that the Son of God is come, and hath given us an understanding, that we may know him that is true; and we are in him that is true, even in his Son Jesus Christ. This is the true God and eternal life."

The *memory* will not be idle, or useless, in this blessed work. From that height the saint can look behind him and before him. And to compare past with present things must raise in the blessed soul an inconceivable esteem and sense of its condition. To stand on that mount, whence we can see the wilderness and Canaan both at once; to stand in heaven and look back on earth, and weigh them together in the balance of a comparing sense and judgment, how must it needs transport the soul, and make it cry out.

But, O! the full, the near, the sweet enjoyment, is that of *love*. "God is love, and he that dwelleth in love dwelleth in God, and God in him." Now the poor soul complains, "O that I could love Christ more!" Then thou canst not but love him. Now, thou knowest little of amiableness and therefore lovest little: then, thine eyes will affect thy heart, and the continual viewing of that perfect beauty will keep thee in continual transport of love. Christian, doth it not now stir up your love to remember all the experiences of his love? Doth not kindness melt you, and the sunshine of divine goodness warm your frozen hearts? What will it do then, when you shall live in love, and have all in him, who is all? Surely love is both work and wages. What a high favor, that God will give us leave to love him! But more than this, he returneth love for love; nay, a thousand times more. Christian, thou wilt be then brimful of love; yet, love as much as thou canst, thou shalt be ten thousand times more beloved. Were the arms of the Son of God open upon the cross, and an open passage made to his heart by the spear; and will not his arms and heart be open to thee in glory? Did not he begin to love before thou lovedst, and will not he continue now? Did he love thee, an enemy? thee, a sinner? thee, who even loathedst thyself? and own thee, when thou didst disclaim thyself? And will he not now immeasurably love thee, a son? thee, a perfect saint? thee, who returnest some love for love? He that in love wept over the old Jerusalem when near its ruin, with what love will he rejoice over the new Jerusalem in her glory!

Christian, believe this, and think on it: thou shalt be eternally embraced in the arms of that love which was from everlasting, and will extend to everlasting; of that love which brought the Son of God's love from heaven to earth, from earth to the cross, from the cross to the grave, from the grave to glory; that love which was weary, hungry, tempted, scorned, scourged, buffeted, spit upon, crucified, pierced; which did fast, pray, teach, heal, weep, sweat, bleed, die; that love will eternally embrace thee. Know this, believe, to thy everlasting comfort, if those arms have once embraced thee, neither sin nor hell can get thee thence for ever. Thou hast not to deal with an inconstant creature, but with him with whom is no variableness nor shadow of turning. Indeed thou mayest be "persuaded that neither death nor life, nor angels, nor principalities, nor powers, nor things present, nor things to come, nor height, nor depth, nor any other creature, shall be able to separate us from the love of God which is in

Christ Jesus our Lord." And now, are we not left in the apostle's admiration: "What shall we say to these things?" Infinite love must needs be mystery to a finite capacity. No wonder angels desire to look into this mystery. And if it be the study of saints here "to know the breadth, and length, and depth, and height of the love of Christ, which passeth knowledge"; the saints' everlasting rest must consist in the enjoyment of God by love.

Nor does *joy* share least in this fruition. It is this which all we have mentioned lead to, and conclude in; even the inconceivable complacency which the blessed feel in seeing, knowing, loving, and being beloved of God. This is "the white stone which no man knoweth, saving he that receiveth it." All Christ's ways of mercy tend to and end in the saints' joys. He wept, sorrowed, suffered, that they might rejoice; he sends the Spirit to be their comforter; he multiplies promises; he discovers their future happiness, that their joy may be full. He opens to them the fountain of living waters, that they may thirst no more, and that it may spring up in them to everlasting life. He chastens them that he may give them rest. He makes it their duty to rejoice in him always, and again commands them to rejoice. He never brings them into so low a condition that he does not leave them more cause of joy than sorrow. And hath the Lord such a care of our comfort here? O what will that joy be where, the soul being perfectly prepared for joy and joy prepared by Christ for the soul, it shall be our work, our business, eternally to rejoice! It seems the saints' joy shall be greater than the damned's torment; for their torment is the torment of creatures, prepared for the devil and his angels; but our joy is the joy of our Lord. The same glory which the Father gave the Son, the Son hath given them, to sit with him in his throne, even as he is set down with his Father in his throne. Thou, poor soul, who prayest for joy, waitest for joy; complainest for want of joy, longest for joy; thou then shalt have full joy, as much as thou canst hold, and more than ever thou thoughtest on, or thy heart desired. In the meantime walk carefully, watch constantly, and then let God measure out to thee thy times and degrees of joy. It may be he keeps them until thou hast more need. Thou hadst better lose thy comfort than thy safety. If thou shouldst die full of fears and sorrows, it will be but a moment, and they are all gone and concluded in joy inconceivable. As the joy of the hypocrite, so the fears of the upright are but for a moment. God's "anger endureth but a moment; in his favor is life; weeping may endure for a night, but joy cometh in the morning." O blessed morning! Poor, humble, drooping soul, how would it fill thee with joy now, if a voice from heaven should tell thee of the love of God, the pardon of thy sins, and assure thee of thy part in these joys! What then will thy joy be, when thy actual possession shall convince thee of thy title, and thou shalt be in heaven before thou art well aware!

And it is not thy joy only; it is a *mutual joy* as well as a mutual love. Is there joy in heaven at thy conversion, and will there be none at thy glorification? Will not the angels welcome thee thither, and congratulate thy safe arrival? Yes, it is the joy of Jesus Christ; for now he hath the end of his undertaking, labor, suffering, dying, when we have our joys; when he is "glorified in his Saints, and admired in all them that believe"; when he "sees of the travail of his soul, and is satisfied." This is Christ's harvest, when he shall reap the fruit of his labors; and it will not repent him concerning his sufferings, but he will rejoice over his purchased inheritance, and his people will rejoice in him. Yea, the Father himself puts on joy, too, in our joy. As we grieve his Spirit and weary him with our iniquities, so he is rejoiced in our good. O how quickly does he now spy a returning prodigal, even afar off! How does he run and meet him! And with what compassion does he fall on his neck and kiss him, and put on him the best robe, and a ring on his hand, and shoes on his feet, and kills the fatted calf, to eat and be merry! This is indeed a happy meeting; but nothing to the embracing and joy of that last and great meeting. Yea, more; as God doth mutually love and joy, so he makes this his rest, as it is our rest. What an eternal Sabbatism, when the work of redemption, is all finished and perfected for ever! "The Lord thy God in the midst of thee is mighty; he will save, he will rejoice over thee with joy, he will rest in his love, he will rest in his love, he will joy over thee with singing." Well may we then rejoice in our God with joy, and rest in our love, and joy in him with singing.

Alas! my fearful heart scarce dares proceed. Methinks I hear the Almighty's voice saying to me, "Who is this that darkeneth counsel by words without knowledge?" But pardon thy servant, O Lord. I have not pried into unrevealed things. I bewail that my apprehensions are so dull, my thoughts so mean, my affections so stupid, and my expressions so low and unbecoming such a glory. I have only heard by the hearing of the ear: O let thy servant see thee, and possess these joys; then shall I have more suitable conceptions, and shall give thee fuller glory; I shall abhor my present self, and disclaim and renounce all these imperfections. "I have uttered that I understood not, things too wonderful for me, which I knew not." Yet "I believe, and therefore have I spoken." What, Lord, canst thou expect from dust, but levity? or from corruption, but defilement? Though the weakness and irreverence be the fruit of my own corruption, yet the fire is from thine altar, and the work of thy commanding. I looked not into thy ark, nor put forth my hand unto it without thee. Wash away these stains also in the blood of the Lamb. Imperfect or none must be thy service here. O take thy Son's excuse, "the spirit is willing, but the flesh is weak."

(Adapted)

Heaven is Our Home

JAMES THOMPSON

For we have not here an abiding city, but we seek after the city which is to come. — Heb. 13:14.

THE Hebrew Christians had many trials to encounter, many losses to meet. In consequence of their professed attachment to Christ they were driven away from their habitation and were compelled to go elsewhere; but this must not tempt them to renounce their faith and hope. Their permanent dwelling-place, they must remember, is not on earth but in Heaven. The City of Jerusalem, however dear to them because of its sacred associations and hallowed memories was not the abiding city. The Saviour had been led out of Jerusalem and was put to death that He might sanctify the people with His own blood; and they should be willing to leave its gates behind them, to be exiled from the city where they dwelt and made wanderers in the earth, for their permanent home is not anywhere in the world. They are but pilgrims and sojourners: let them seek an abiding city, the one that is to come, the new Jerusalem. They might have used such words as these: —

> "Though painful and distressing,
> Yet there's a rest above;
> And onward still we're pressing
> To reach the land of love."

Although our circumstances are so different in several respects from those of the Hebrews, the words of our text have an application for us also. Change and decay in all around we see, yet the human heart clings to its longing for the unchanging and eternal.

I. Let us consider, first, THE WANT OF PERMANENCE IN THE PRESENT ORDER OF THINGS. The fashion of the world passeth away, becometh something quite different from what it was. The things around us have no permanence; they continue not in one stay. In this world of ours everything is fleeting and evanescent, like the glory of the morning's dawn or the beauty of the evening's sunset.

We ourselves are subject to many changes. We are surrounded by change in every form, and the time comes when we pass away and disappear from the visible world. Our circumstances in life are characterized by mutability. In some cases the extremes of fortune are experienced in the short span of a lifetime. If we think of what we are told of Joseph we remember how his early years were clouded by calamity after calamity, and how subsequently he rose to be Prime Minister of Egypt. If we think of David we find him sounding the whole gamut of human experience. You have merely to employ your own observation and recall your own experience to be convinced that changes are incident to humanity, that life is disturbed by many a shock, is agitated by many a storm of sorrow, severed friendships, broken relationships, wounded affections.

> "This is the state of man; to-day he puts forth
> The tender leaves of hope, to-morrow blossoms,
> And bears his blushing honours thick upon him,
> The third day comes a frost, a killing frost,
> And — when he thinks, good easy man, full surely
> His greatness is ripening — nips his root
> And then he falls."

Possessions come and go; worldly means may increase or diminish; sanguine hopes may be largely realized or woefully disappointed. In any case our lives are subjected to many a vicissitude and are shaken in various ways until at length the bodily frame is reduced to weakness, decay and dissolution.

There is a story told of a king who stood one day looking on a magnificent procession which was passing by. It was a most imposing spectacle. Turning to one of his attendants the king exclaimed with a feeling of satisfaction and pride: "Is it not perfectly glorious?" The attendant made to this inquiry a striking reply: "It lacks one thing, your majesty, to make it perfect." "And what is that?" asked the king. The answer given was, "Continuance." The same may be said of every worldly possession, of every earthly pageant, of human life itself: it lacks continuance.

Man's pride has endeavoured to set this law at defiance and to erect or construct something that would have the elements of permanence. In Egypt, Assyria, India and China such attempts were made, and the monuments of those gigantic efforts have survived the centuries. The most solid of empires have declined and fallen. Man's most heroic efforts to triumph over the enormous power of change prove abortive. All the great empires of antiquity are gone, are shorn of their ancient pomp and might. All that the world is proud of and glories in grows dim and dies. Even what has been called the "unchanging East" must pass through its revolutions, as we have seen in our own time. The law of ceaseless change affects all things that are present and visible; and history is but a record of the fact and power of this law, a series of pictures of epochs and vicissitudes.

Transiency is written upon everything here, and we ourselves are passing away. We are not fixtures here, and the things around us are not fixtures. There is nothing stable or immutable beneath the evershifting skies. We are all of us in one way or another under the unalterable necessity of change. This is the absolute condition of existence here and now. All things fade or pass into something else. A poet has reminded us that

"This world is all a fleeting show
    For man's illusion given;
The smiles of joy, the tears of woe,
Deceitful shine, deceitful flow, —
    There's nothing true but heaven.

And false the light on glory's plume,
    As fading hues of even,
And love and hope and beauty's bloom,
Are garlands gather'd for the tomb. —
    There's nothing bright but heaven."

There is nothing true, abiding, reliable, but the great eternal verities, those things which the everlasting Gospel brings to view. A man is not sure of his property, his money, his children. It might seem as if we could reckon upon such possessions as lasting at least our day; but they may not. Edmund Burke's exclamation, when news reached him of the sudden death of a fellow-candidate and colleague, has been often quoted. The great statesman, when he heard the startling tidings amid the excitement and contests of public life, uttered the memorable words: "What shadows we are and what shadows we pursue!" And said one who lived in the far distant past: "Our days are as a shadow, and there is none abiding."

II. The question now arises as to How WE SHOULD FEEL ABOUT THE FACT OF LIFE'S CHANGES AND TRANSIENCY. How shall we meet it when we fully grasp it and see it with the inner eye of the mind? It may bring bitterness and sadness, or blessedness and hope. It may add darkness or impart brightness to life. Man will be impressed and influenced by it in some way. Some realizing the transitory nature of all earthly things may become gloomy and depressed, may cease to strive, may yield to despair, may resign themselves to the inevitable in the spirit of indifference and indolence.

Others may become reckless and sensual. Since life is so short, since its good things are so uncertain and so short-lived, they abandon themselves to pleasure, self-indulgence and vice, like those who said: "Let us eat and drink, for to-morrow we die."

> "Some there be that shadows kiss;
> Such have but a shadow's bliss."

Others, again, as they think that here they have no abiding city, may be inspired with a glorious hope. They turn away their minds from the downward gaze and raise their thoughts to the throne and the eternal love of God. Thus a hope, like sunshine through an April shower, brightens the life which were otherwise so fleeting and sad, so flat and unprofitable.

In other words, men may meet the fact of change and vicissitude wisely or foolishly, with thoughtlessness and self-gratification or with the serious consideration due to one of the great facts of human life. How does the Bible teach us to think and feel about this truth which frequently comes upon men with such suddenness, and with such force? It tells us of a living hope, a hope full of immortality. It assures us that beyond the shadows there are eternal realities; it tells us of a city that abides, a city which the Christian pilgrim eagerly looks forward to and which he will one day succeed in reaching. He is thus encouraged and sustained amid earth's buffetings by the hope of the Gospel.

> "Earth is brightened when that gleam
> Falls on flower and rock and stream;
> Life is brightened when that ray
> Falls upon its darkest day."

III. This brings us to the CHRISTIAN FAITH AND HOPE. We seek a city that is to come and one that will abide. We are looking for something that will continue, something that will never pass away and will never mock us. This faith, this hope is based upon what we know of God, the Eternal and Unchanging One, and of His unfailing promises. He remains ever the same amid the fluctuation of the things that are seen and the alternations of life and death. Through time and change and death His truth endures and His Kingdom stands.

In Christ we have a triumphant hope. He has brought life and immortality to light. There is a glorious inheritance beyond for His followers; hence amid their daily duties, their difficulties and perplexities, they do not forget the glory that is to be revealed. Perhaps some Christians in the present time have not as much of this spirit as they ought and hold not the primitive hope in anything like its primitive strength. If they could grasp it more firmly it would be an immense gain and incentive. It would not make them false to their duties in this world, but it would give them the victory over the world.

When Stanley was in the awful tropical forest, spending weary months in its gloom, assailed by enemies and threatened by many dangers there was one thing that kept up his courage and prevented his patience from giving way. What was this? It was his strong conviction that the gloomy forest was not endless, but was encircled by light, and that the day of rest and relief would surely come. In like manner when there is a strong assurance of the continuing city, when the day breaks and the shadows flee away, it will be a motive-power which will lift us above many a fear and grief, which even amid darkness and distress will make us patient, strong and hopeful.

On the other hand, if men get to think that there is room to doubt and deny the reality of the abiding city, that after all God may leave them in the dust and may mock all their yearnings and aspirations, what effect would such a thought have upon their life and character? A few noble spirits, to be sure, might combine with such a belief earnestness of purpose and usefulness of life, but to the great majority it would be vastly otherwise. Many, it is to be feared, would lose all sense of the sacredness of life and its solemn responsibilities; they would fling it away when any serious inconvenience arose; they would cease to reverence themselves as made in the image of God. Existence here would come to be a poor, dwarfed, stunted, miserable thing; its glory would have vanished.

"O life as futile then as frail."

But think of the Christian conception founded on the love of God in Jesus Christ our Lord. To those who believe in Chirst's victory over the grave, death is not a mystery, is not a dark cloud toward which all are moving and in which all must sooner or later be lost sight of. They look at life and death in their true proportions and relations. They have no shrinking fear of that undiscovered country from whose bourne no traveller returns. For them death has been abolished, and while they may desire to abide as long as possible in the body, they know that to depart is to be with Christ and enjoy clearer light and fuller blessedness.

"We know," wrote the Apostle Paul, "that if our earthly house of this tabernacle were dissolved, we have a building of God, an house not made with hands, eternal in the heavens." He was assured of a building reserved for him far more substantial than the frail, moving tent in which his soul then abode. "We know."

This accent of certainty was characteristic of the early Christian writers, and is in contrast with the hesitating, doubtful spirit found not infrequently in recent times. Life for believers now has become a more pleasant thing than it was in the apostolic age. It is now free from persecution, involves no material loss, brands no one with a stigma of reproach, and the result is in some instances at least that the Christian faith has lost somewhat of its reality, heaven has become more shadowy, the powers of the world to come are not felt as they ought to be.

What is there that will in any degree counteract this weakening of faith and hope? The contemplation of Jesus Christ — what He is and what He has done — and of the glory in which He now dwells will accomplish much in this direction. When He becomes real and precious to anyone, the unseen world is grasped, the influences of his grace encircle the life and the great realities of the future exert their power over the present. If we could look at earth through the glasses of eternity, its prizes and pleasures, the things that now seem so great and so indispensable would dwindle into insignificance. If Christ were a reality to us, our affections would be set on things above, we should live as strangers and pilgrims here, we should keep our faces heavenward and live as those whose citizenship is in Heaven.

> "For ah! the Master is so fair,
>   His smile so sweet on banished men,
> That they who meet it unaware,
>   Can never turn to earth again.
>
> And they who see Him risen far
>   At God's right hand to welcome them,
> Forgetful stand of home and land
>   Desiring fair Jerusalem."

In Northern India there is a spacious city built by a Mogul Emperor for his own glory. It is now absolutely deserted by men. There is a vast gate-way in the silent walls, and over it there is carved an Arabic inscription which, wonderful to relate, purports to preserve an utterance of Jesus not found in the New Testament. It is a striking saying and worthy of note:

> "Jesus on Whom be peace hath said,
> This world is but a bridge; pass over;
> But build not thy dwelling there."

This is the proper way to use the world, passing over it as a bridge, earnest and occupied all the way, yet with heart and hope ever looking forward to the life of the world to come. Seeing that we belong to an order of things doomed to change and decay, seeing that we ourselves are so frail, we should realize that our blessedness consists in being united to God through Jesus Christ, the unchanging, ever-abiding Saviour. Thus we secure a permanent, an eternal life. And no shocks of time, no blows of circumstance, not even death itself can injure the life that is hid with Christ in God. May He in His infinite mercy grant to each of us this enduring substance. Amen.

II. Brief Sermons and Meditations

WORDS OF COMFORT FOR AFFLICTED PARENTS
(I Cor. 13:12)

In casting about for what might be suitable at such a time as this, and under such trying circumstances, there came the thought that the limitations of the present life are so great that we understand its meaning and destiny very imperfectly. For what is there that these parents would more earnestly desire than to have the children God gives them spared unto them, to the end that they may grow up to be useful men and honorable women — the joy and comfort of their hearts? I do not say that these Christian parents — now that Providence has taken from them their dear daughter — would wish to bring her back contrary to the will of God. They have, doubtless, received grace from God to pray: "Thy will be done."

But it is often the case that our hearts are so set upon our children that we desire, by all means, to retain them, and are quite unreconciled when they are taken from us. The number, perhaps, is rather small of those who are able sincerely to say: "The Lord gave, and the Lord hath taken away: blessed be the name of the Lord!" Now, murmurings arise from two sources: first, from our lack of grace; and, second, from defective means of vision. With more grace we should have more resignation. With clearer vision we should have more desire to depart and be with Jesus, and more cheerful submission to the will of God when He takes our dear ones to Himself.

I. DEFICIENCIES IN OUR VISION.

The Apostle declares that "now we see through a glass, darkly." These limitations of vision are both natural and spiritual. Organs of sight have been given us for seeing the natural world, and intelligence to enable us to look within material things, to discern what is underneath their surface and discover their meaning and philosophy. But notice how these which serve us best — the senses and reason — come far short of perfection; up to a certain extent they serve us all alike. We see, in common with all animals, what is upon the surface of things — and the outward world looks alike to all of us; but the moment we try to look within, one man sees one thing, another another, and we have almost as many philosophies as there are minds.

For spiritual things faith is given us. And yet even through this noble eye of the soul, "we see through a glass, darkly." We see darkly through the dispensations of Providence. Many are its unsolved mysteries. Those dispensations that are favorable, we gladly accept and question lightly; but those that are afflictive we sadly accept, would gladly thrust them from us, and are at a loss how to understand or interpret them. But we still further see darkly through the glories and realities of the heavenly life and the full happiness of those who are gathered there.

When we contemplate death and behold its masterpiece, the lifeless body of your dear child, we look almost entirely from the standpoint of what it has done for us. And what is this? Death has destroyed a wonderful organization, and broken up a co-partnership between body, soul, and spirit. In doing all this it has separated from us a living form and loving presence. The dear daughter shall never return to us. Death never restores to us those upon whom he has laid his icy hand.

II. Is There Any Remedy for Our Heavy Affliction?

1. *We should seek after larger measures of grace.* Thanks be to God, "we may come boldly unto the throne of grace, that we may obtain mercy, and find grace to help in time of need." If we so do, our grief shall last only through a night, and joy shall come in the morning. Is it nothing that you have a child in heaven? Are the consolations of God small with thee? God does not stint us in the bestowment of grace, but He gives no more than we use. To him that uses shall be given, and he shall have more abundantly.

2. *We should look at what death has been instrumental in ac-complishing for the child.* And what is this? Death has re-moved her from all the uncertainty, sickness, pain, sorrow, and change that belong even to the brightest and happiest life here on earth. Through the gateway of death her spirit has ascended to God, who gave it. She is now a full sharer in the glorified bliss of heaven. She dwells where Jesus is, and in full posses-sion of eternal life. Oh, if we could only see more clearly the place she occupies in heaven, the grand capacities and possibili-ties of life opened to her, her early removal from us would have

in it less of anguish and more of consolation! Today, clad in
garments whiter than the snow, she sings with sweeter voice
than has e'er been heard upon earth, and bears a vocal part in
that grand symphony of heaven: "Unto Him that loved us, and
washed us from our sins in His own blood, and hath made us
kings and priests unto God and His Father: to Him be glory
and dominion forever and ever. Amen." — LEWIS O. THOMP-
SON.

THE SHUNAMITE AND HER SON (II Kings 4:26)

This story has soothed the spirit of many a parent, and is still
fraught with consolation. The story suggests:

I. THE SHUNAMITE, THOUGH A GODLY PERSON, WAS NOT
EXEMPT FROM FAMILY BEREAVEMENT. She had one on whom
her affections centered, and who was dear to her, even as her
own soul. To him she clung as one of the chief sources of her
enjoyment, and as one whose life seemed indispensable to her
own. Yet in accordance with the sovereign purpose of God, she
was called to part with this child. In the morning he is with
her and she delights to look upon his opening charms and to
indulge in fond anticipations of the future. At noon he is struck
down by the hand of death, and is no longer hers. "When the
child was grown, etc."

A visitation like that of the Shunamite, is not uncommon with
the people of God. The grim messenger enters their dwelling
and commits his ravages on those whom they love. Darkness
forthwith covers their tabernacle and the cheerful household
hum is hushed. This is the law of nature acting according to the
appointment of God — "By one man, etc." When parents see
their tender flowers blighted and cut down, it well becomes them
to think of sin, as that which brought death into the world and
all our woe. But when they think of death through the first
man, they may think of life through the second man Christ Jesus.

II. THE SHUNAMITE, THOUGH A PIOUS WOMAN, WAS DEEP-
LY GRIEVED BY THE LOSS OF HER CHILD. When Elisha saw her,
he saw grief depicted on her countenance; and when he saw
Gehazi annoyed her with his importunity, his language was, "Let
her alone, for her soul is vexed within her." And why should
not Christians grieve for the loss of their dear children? It is
only when grief becomes immoderate, or when mourning is accompanied by murmuring, that it is offensive to God. It is chief-
ly because bereavements awaken sorrow, that they lead us to see

our need of God and to seek for satisfaction from higher sources than the world with all its transient joys.

III. THE SHUNAMITE AMIDST HER AFFLICTION, BETOOK HERSELF TO GOD. Elisha was not only a man of God but a prophet signally attested by Jehovah. In a certain sense he was the medium of intercourse between God and man. To him the Shunamite came in this her hour of need — unbosomed all her sorrow and looked for the consolation she required. The restoration of the child seemed needful to the realization of the promise that had been made to her. The Christian parent should go to God in the season of bereavement. "He knows our frame," sympathizes, pours the balm of consolation into the wounded spirit. He does not afflict willingly, has gracious designs, assures that afflictions "yield the peaceable fruits of righteousness unto them which are exercised thereby." He leads forth by the right way.

IV. THE SHUNAMITE ACQUIESCED IN THE BEREAVING DISPENSATION, PAINFUL THOUGH IT WAS. When Gehazi met her and accosted her in those courteous terms . . . "Is it well with the child? She answered, It is well." True, her beloved child had been removed from her; after a short, but severe conflict with trouble he had closed his eyes in death. And as a consequence of this her tender heart was wrung with anguish and her soul was vexed within her. But still she could say "it is well." She saw the hand of her God and Father in the trying dispensation, and, like Job, she bowed with holy submission knowing that all was truth and mercy sure. It should not require many words to persuade bereaved parents, that with them also it is well.

Fond parent, look to thy child in its glorified state, for "of such is the kingdom of heaven." Think of him as raised above all sorrow, suffering, and imperfection, and mingling with the innumerable company of the redeemed.

> "Forgive, blest shade, the tributary tear,
>   That mourns thine exit from a world like this:
>   Forgive the wish that would have kept thee here,
>   And stayed thy progress to the realms of bliss."
> — JOHN BRUCE.

SUNSET AT NOON (Jer. 15:9)

Whatever may be the literal meaning of these words they suggest a departure in mid-life. Wherever we go, over land or sea, death's ravages are seen, and at whatever season of the year or hour of the day we visit the abodes of men death has preceded us. It has its types in fading flower, in withering grass, in falling leaf and setting sun.

The sun going down at noon is very suggestive of the unexpectedness of death in the meridian of life, and yet

I. THE SUN GOES DOWN BY THE APPOINTMENT OF GOD. "He maketh night and day," and ruleth the heavens. Joshua and Hezekiah alone have interfered with the sun's course during a period of nearly 6,000 years. To God belong the issues of even death. He never visits without the Divine appointment.

II. THE SUN GOES DOWN FOR THE BENEFIT OF THE HUMAN RACE, that many may retire and rest and recruit his wasted powers, that other portions of the human family may obtain light and heat, and that man's fund of knowledge may be increased. For darkness shows us worlds by night we never saw by day.

So death works for the world's good, restrains wickedness, solemnizes thoughtless ones, though tears and bereavements shadows earth, attracts to heaven and reveals wondrous things to the dead.

III. THE SUN OFTEN GOES DOWN TOO SOON FOR US. Work unfinished, Joshua, Hezekiah, David; "Spare me," Voltaire, Elizabeth. In spite of life's trials and sorrow, we cling to it; even Moses desired to live longer than he might enjoy more of the beauties, but his sun went down on this side of Jordan.

IV. THE SUN HAS HIS NATURAL TIME FOR SETTING. This setting is expected and prepared for by man: to set before would be startling, perplexing, phenomenal. So with human life. Every one expects the accustomed length of day — three score — to be cut off before or in mid-life seems unnatural, abnormal and mysterious.

V. THE SUN GOES DOWN TO RISE AGAIN. In a brief interval he appears again, climbing the heavens in majesty and strength. So with the departed dead. Those in Christ will appear again in golden splendor. Those out of Christ amid the lurid flames of the lost. A time will come when this orb of day will go down, never more to rise, but the godly shall live on, "unhurt," where the "sun shall no more go down."

VI. LET US BE CHEERED BY THIS LIGHT OF REVELATION. God is the Father of Lights, does all things well, and whether the sun of our loved ones depart in the morning, at mid-day, or in the evening, it will have a glorious rising in that perfect day, in which there shall be no night. — W. RODWELL.

THE RIPE CHRISTIAN DYING (Job 5:26)

This is a very beautiful comparison. The shock of corn has passed through many changes, survived many onsets of the worm, and tempests of wind and rain, etc., and is now ripe for the sickle and the garner. So with the aged Christian. How often did he in early life seem likely to be smitten down by death — how often has he been buffetted — accidents innumerable seemed ready to smite — but he has survived and now is bending with weakness and crowned with the glory of the aged Christian. The text intimates:

I. THAT DEATH IS INEVITABLE. "Thou *shalt* come." This is a true saying, and yet how seldom impressed upon the heart. There are many reminders of the fact, but it is usually forgotten. Death is not absolutely necessary to the Christian, for a time will come when "we which are alive and remain shall be caught up," etc.

II. DEATH TO THE CHRISTIAN IS ALWAYS ACCEPTABLE. "Thou shalt *come* to thy grave." There will be a willingness and cheerfulness to die. He shall die quietly, coming to the grave as to a quiet resting-place — this has been the experience of many of God's children.

III. THE CHRISTIAN'S DEATH IS ALWAYS TIMELY. "In a full age." Die when God's children may, they die in "full age." "A full age" is whenever God likes to take his children home. Some fruits ripen early, others late in the season. A Christian will never die too soon, and never die too late — never before ripeness and not after ripeness.

IV. THE CHRISTIAN WILL DIE WITH HONOR. "Like a shock of corn cometh in his season." There is such a thing as an honorable funeral, where devout men assemble, carry to the grave and make great lamentation. Such funerals are like a "harvest home." There is such a melancholy grandeur there. We ought to pay great respect to the departed saint's bodies. "The memory of the just is blessed."

There are two funerals for every Christian; one the funeral of the body and the other the soul — rather it is the marriage of the soul; for angels stand ready to carry it to the Saviour. The angels, imitating husbandmen, as they near the gates of

heaven may shout "Harvest Home." There is a holiday whenever a saint enters — and there is praise to God,

"While life, or thought, or being lasts,
   Or immortality endures."
                           — CHARLES H. SPURGEON.

CHRIST'S RESURRECTION THE PROMISE AND PROPHECY OF OUR OWN (I Cor. 15:20)

I find in the text a prophecy of our resurrection. Before I
finish I hope to pass through every cemetery and drop a flower
of hope on the tombs of all who have died in Christ. Rejoicing
in Christ's resurrection we rejoice in the resurrection of all the
good.

The greatest of all conquerors is not Alexander, or Caesar, or
Napoleon, but *death*. His throne is in the sepulcher. But his
scepter shall be broken, for the dead in Christ shall arise.

There are mysteries around this resurrection of the body which
I can't explain. Who can unravel the mysteries of nature? Who
can explain how this vast variety of flowers have come from
seeds which look so nearly alike? Tell me how God can turn
the chariot of His omnipotence on a rose leaf? Mystery meets
us at every turn.

Objects one: The body may be scattered — an arm in Africa,
a leg in Europe, the rest of the body here. How will it be gathered on the resurrection morn?

Another objects: The body changes every seven years. It is
perishing continually. The blood-vessels are canals along which
the breadstuff is conveyed to the wasted and hungry parts of
our bodies. Says another: A man dies; plants take up parts of
the body; animals eat the plants, and other men eat the animals.
Now, to which body will belong these particles of matter?

Are these all the questions you can ask? If not, ask on. I
do not pretend to answer them. I fall back on these words. "All
that are in their graves shall come forth."

There are some things, however, we do know about the resur-
rected body.

1. It will be a glorious body. The body, as we now see it, is
but a skeleton to what it would have been were it not marred
by sin.

2. It will be an immortal body.

3. A powerful body — unconquerable for evermore — never
tired.

May God fill you today with glorious anticipations! Oh, blessed hope! — T. DeWitt Talmage.

DEATH SWALLOWED UP IN VICTORY (I Cor. 15:54)

There are two evils in death: the personal fear of it, and unconsoled bereavement. Experience of both these is world-wide, and we need deliverance from both. He who is free from heartbreak at the death of others is apt to blench when he himself looks death in the face; and the brave soul who is not afraid to die trembles and agonizes at the death of those he loves.

God, therefore, early began to speak to men about this, and we find the accumulated wisdom of such in Job's friends, and Balaam, and sometimes the higher strains of Isaiah's poetry and Paul's lofty prose.

Paul makes the following points:

I. DEATH MAKES NO BREAK IN NORMAL CHRISTIAN PROGRESS. See I Cor. 15:46-50.

> "There is not Death! What seems so is transition.
> This life of mortal breath
> Is but a suburb of the life elysian,
> Whose portals we call Death."

II. THE CHANGE IS NECESSARY TO PROGRESS.

Home is not destroyed by sending children away to school. The painfulness is in our faulty condition. See I Cor. 15:50-54.

III. THE MEANING OF THE CHANGE APPEARS WHEN WE SEE CHRIST.

What we need is a renewal of character. This comes in the new birth, and the new birth is the apprehension of Christ.

Conclusion. — Are you in the true line of progress? Is this your hope for your children? Is it your own hope- — HOMILETIC REVIEW.

CHRIST'S RESURRECTION THE TYPE OF OURS
(Rom. 6:4)

The sons of Sarephath, Shunem, and Nain were brought back from the dead, as were Lazarus and Eutychus, but these did not at that time share in the resurrection. Their bodies were not changed from corruptible to incorruptible, from mortal to immortal; they were still death's prisoners on parole. But over the risen body of Christ or His disciple, death has no power. Enoch and Elijah were "translated," "changed," like those who are alive at Christ's coming again; mortality was swallowed up of life.

Christ is the first-born of the dead; and His resurrection shows the law and method of ours. The points of resemblance we may indicate.

I. HE ROSE, AS WE SHALL, BY THE POWER OF THE HOLY SPIRIT. — In each period of His life He was dependent upon the Spirit; and the same Spirit who had nestled to His heart in His baptism hovered over the grave in Joseph's garden; and on the third day loosed the pains of death, because it was not possible He should be holden of it. The Holy Spirit forgets no body which has been made His temple. He shall "quicken our mortal bodies."

II. HIS RESURRECTION WAS UNOBTRUSIVE, like all divine work; like the unfolding of flowers. The doors of our tombs will open on noiseless hinges; the fetters will drop lightly from our hands; our bodies will rise into immortal beauty like a dream.

III. HIS RESURRECTION WAS LEISURELY. — The burial-clothes were folded and laid aside, as Christ without haste rose in majesty. God's children shall not go out by flight, for the Lord has gone before them, and His glory shall be their reward.

IV. HIS RESURRECTION WAS IRRESISTIBLE. — When Joseph and Nicodemus left him in the tomb, the guards tried to hold him fast. But God said, and will say for us: "Let my people go."

V. HIS RISEN BODY WAS LIKE HIS MORTAL BODY. — As in the buried seed, the principle of vitality was unchanged. His glorious body was different from the body of his humiliation, yet it was the same. He could vanish and pass through doors, yet they knew him the same. So those that sleep in Jesus become fairer, stronger, swifter, more apt for service, yet wake with the endeared features, familiar tones, and happy companionship.

VI. WHAT CHRIST DOES IN RENEWING OUR SOULS HE WILL YET DO IN RENEWING OUR BODIES.—This will be the top-stone in the edifice of redemption. — F. B. MEYER.

A GLANCE INTO THE WORLD TO COME (Rev. 14:13)

Why are those happy that die in the Lord? Two reasons: "They rest from their labours," and "their works follow them."

"They rest." That is, doubtless, a happiness which is something negative, but which is none the less of great value. Who does not know by experience what sweetness there is in rest coming after fatigue? The present life is every moment a fatigue, from which death is an eternal rest; rest from labour, rest from sufferings, rest from sin.

But the happiness of those who have died in the Lord is not merely negative. They are not only freed from the fatigues and the trials of life, they enjoy a boundless felicity. That is what the Holy Spirit declares in our text, when it is said that "their works follow them."

There exists a close connection between the present life and the life to come; the latter is, as it were, the continuation and the accomplishment of the former; the character of the life to come is determined in the case of each one by that of his present life. His faith bears its fruits in that other life, and it is changed into sight; he contemplates and he touches what he had believed. Here below, he saw the truth confusedly, and as through an obscure medium; but, sustained by faith, he advanced in peace in the midst of the perplexities of life; he waited with patience the great day of revelations; he accepted as good and full of love dispensations which he understood not. And now, to recompense his faith, he sees face to face; every veil is removed, all obscurities dissipated. To his view, which is illuminated from on high, the whole of the magnificent plan of God towards the world is all unfolded, and everywhere he discovers wonders of wisdom and of love. The most unsearchable, the most painful dispensations of the present life appear to him in the life to come the wisest and most paternal; and who can tell the transports of admiration and of holy joy into which that revelation of the ways of God casts him! His submission to the Divine will follow him equally after death; it bears its fruit in the life to come, and it is changed into happiness.

It is very little to say that he is for ever delivered from the trials of every kind; these trials give place not only to rest, but to unspeakable enjoyments. We have said how the works of the people of God become after their death elements of their felicity; but there is yet another sense in which it can be said that these works follow them in eternal life. Their works still follow them in this sense, that they continue in heaven that life of devotedness to the Saviour, and of activity for his service, which they commenced on earth. The happiness of heaven will not be a barren inaction; it will be an essentially active happiness. They will take part, in a manner which we cannot picture here below, in the work of God and in the government of the universe; perhaps each of them will have, as here below, special aptitudes, which God will make the most of, by assigning to each of them particular occupations in harmony with these aptitudes. In order to be able to apply the promises of my text, we must therefore die in the Lord.

1. To die in the Lord is, in the first place, *to die in the faith of the Lord;* it is to renounce all hope of salvation founded on ourselves, on our works, on our pretended merits, and to cause our hopes to rest only on the merits of Christ, on the atonement accomplished by his blood.

2. To die in the Lord is also *to die in the love of the Lord;* it is to love Him Who loved us first, and that unto the Cross; it is to feel ourselves drawn to him by an intimate and powerful affection; it is, when dying, to be able to say with St. Paul; "I have a desire to depart, and be with Christ, which is far better."

3. To die in the Lord is once *more to die in obedience to the Lord.* It is to die after having lived here below in imitation of Jesus; after having purified ourselves as he also is pure; it is to have lived, I do not say in a state of perfect holiness, but at least in the constant desire of holiness, making continual efforts to reach it, and approaching it more and more.

4. In fine, and to say all in one single word, to die in the Lord is to *die in communion with the Lord;* it is to die, after having lived, dead to the world and to sin, with a life "hid with Christ in God." — H. MONOD.

THE GREAT CHANGE (I Cor. 15:53)

The apostle presents this —

I. AS A CONTRAST BETWIXT WHAT MAN NOW IS AND WHAT HE WILL BE.

1. Twice over the apostle affirms the change from corruptible to incorruption, and from mortal to immortality; first as a matter of necessity, then as a matter of fact. Four times over, also, he uses the same word, translated "put on," which means, to "go into," as into a place of covering or shelter; and hence to go into one's clothes, to attire, to array one's self or others in garments, ornaments, or the like (2 Cor. v. 2).

2. Death, then, is a mere "unclothing" of the man, and if there is any propriety in the analogy the "unclothing" leaves him in possession of the full integrity of his being: He has simply stripped off his garments, and for a season laid them aside. It is still competent for him to resume them, or to array himself in different attire; and on reinvestment he cannot be other than

he was before. Very great may the change be betwixt the "clothing" before death and that which is "put on" at the resurrection, but the language of the apostle implies that its use and purpose in both cases are the same.

3. Then, again, the apostle informs us, twice over, that that which in the one state is corruptible and mortal, becomes in the other state incorruptible and immortal. The thing is the same in both states, but placed under different conditions. At present it is organized matter, liable to decay, injury, and dissolution; but that same organized matter will be found in a state of "incorruption" and "immortality."

II. AS A VICTORY OVER DEATH AND THE GRAVE.

1. The words mean properly "unto victory"; the idea being that the process of extermination goes on like a battle that is waged until a triumphant victory is secured — that is, "aye and until" death is totally abolished. Death at the resurrection is destined to be cast, like a stone, into an abyss, so profound that it never will be brought up or appear again.

2. Death is compared to a venomous reptile which has wounded its victims and introduced into their body its deadly poison. Dissolution, it is true, does not immediately follow the implanting of the sting, but there is pain and anguish, and death ensues in due course of time. And then comes the victory of the grave, or Hades. Like a resistless conqueror, it lays hold of those whom death has prostrated, consigns the body to the house appointed for all living, and the soul to the mysterious condition of disembodied consciousness. Well may this be called a victory, for nothing can be conceived of as a more complete overthrow of human hopes and desires; but introduce the idea of resurrection and it is plain the victory passes over to the other side. The conqueror is despoiled of his triumph; and from being a victim, sin-ruined and dying man, restored to that high standard of corporeal life for which he was originally designed, is in his turn a conqueror, all the more distinguished and glorious that his triumph lasts for ever.

III. AS A BOON FOR WHICH GRATITUDE OUGHT TO BE FELT AND THANKS RETURNED.

Gratitude is the appropriate sequel of benefits bestowed and appreciated. But to realize to the full the emotion of gratitude of which the apostle here speaks, we must actually close with and appropriate the glorious boon. This is the office of faith. None are excluded from the offers of the gospel: all are invited to partake of its blessed privileges; and however great and precious these privileges may be, so far as the present world is concerned, the actual consummation is the resurrection of the body and a portion in the kingdom of God. When the wilderness journey was over, and the wars of the settlement in Canaan at an end, how gladsome would every household be and every heart in Israel as they sat down each one under his vine and fig-tree, and none to make them afraid! But this was only a type of far more glorious things to come, when the epoch of sorrow and death is over, and the entire company of God's redeemed enters upon the long-promised inheritance. — J. COCHRANE.

THE STING OF DEATH EXTRACTED (I Cor. 15:55)

The reason I like the gospel is that it has taken out of my path the worst enemies I ever had. My mind goes back to twenty years ago, before I was converted and I think very often how dark it used to seem at times as I thought of the future. There was death! what a terrible enemy it seemed! I was brought up in a little village in New England. It was the custom there when a person was buried to toll out the age of the man at his funeral. I used to count the strokes of the bell. Death never entered that village, and tore away one of the inhabitants, but I always used to count the tolling of the bell. Sometimes it would be away up to seventy, or between seventy and eighty; beyond the life allotted to man, when man seemed living on borrowed time when cut off. Sometimes it would be clear down in the teens and childhood, for death had taken away one of my own age. It used to make a solemn impression on me; I used to be a great coward. When it comes to death, some men say, "I do not fear it." I feared it, and felt terribly afraid when I thought of being launched into eternity, to go to an unknown world. I used to have dreadful thoughts of God; but they are all gone now. Death has lost its sting. And as I go on through the world I can shout now, when the bell is tolling, "O death, where is thy sting?" And I hear a voice come rolling down from Calvary: "Buried in the bosom of the Son of God." He robbed death of its sting; He took away the sting of death when He gave His own bosom to the stroke. — D. L. MOODY.

VICTORY OVER DEATH (I Cor. 15:56, 57)

I. THE TERRORS OF THE DYING HOUR.

That which makes it peculiarly terrible to die is asserted here to be guilt. It is not the only sting of death, but it contains the venom of the most exquisite torture. It is no mark of courage to speak lightly of dying. There is a world of untold sensations crowded into that moment when a man puts his hand to his forehead and feels the damp upon it which tells him his hour is come. He had been looking for death all his life, and now it is come; it is all over: his chance is past, and his eternity is settled. It is a mockery to speak lightly of that which we cannot know till it comes.

1. *Every living thing instinctively cleaves to its own experience.* It is the first and intensest desire of living things *to be.* It is in virtue of this unquenchable impulse that the world, in spite of all the misery that is in it, continues to struggle on. What are war and trade and labor and professions? Are they the result of struggling to be great? No; they are the result of the struggle *to be.* Reduce the nation or the man to the last resources, and only see what marvellous energy of contrivance the love of being arms them with. Read back the pauper's history at the end of seventy years, and learn what he has done to hold his being where everything is against him, and the only conceivable charm of whose existence is that it *is* existence. Talk as we will of immortality, there is an obstinate feeling that we end in death; and *that* may be felt together with the firmest belief in resurrection. Our faith tells us one thing; our sensations, another.

2. *It is the parting from all around which are twined the heart's best affections.* We become wedded to the sights and sounds of this lovely world more and more closely as years go on. When Lot quitted Sodom, the younger members of the family went on gladly; it was the aged one who looked behind to the home which had so many recollections connected with it. Every time the sun sets, every time the old man sees his children gathering around him, there is a filling of the eye with an emotion we can understand.

3. *The sensation of loneliness attaches to death.* Have we ever seen a ship preparing to sail, with its load of pauper emigrants, to a distant colony? All beyond the seas, to the ignorant poor man, is an unknown land. There comes upon him a sensation new and inexpressibly miserable — the feeling of being alone in the world. So we go on our dark, mysterious journey, for the first time in all our existence, without one to accompany us. Friends are beside our bed; they must stay behind. We die alone. Grant that the Christian has something like a familiarity with the Most High — that breaks this solitary feeling. But for the mass of men

there is no one point in all eternity on which the eye can fix distinctly and rest gladly.

4. *The sting of death is sin.* There are two ways in which this truth applies itself. Some carry about with them the dreadful secret of certain sin that has been committed, guilt that has a name. They have injured some one, made money by unfair means, been unchaste, or done some one of the thousand things which leave a dark spot upon the heart. They shut them out, but it will not do. When a guilty man begins to think of dying, it is like a vision of the Son of Man calling out all the voices of the unclean spirits: "Art thou come to torment us before the time?"

But with most men it is not guilty acts, but *guiltiness of heart* that weighs the heaviest. It is just this feeling: "God is not my friend; I am going on to my grave, and no *man* can say aught against me, but my heart is not right. It is not so much what I have done; it is what I am. Who shall save me from myself?" But let us bear in mind that this sting of sin is not constant. We may live many years before a death in our family forces the thought of death personally home — many years before the quick, short cough, lassitude, emaciation, pain, come upon us in our young vigor and make us feel what it is to be here with death inevitable. And when these symptoms become habitual, habit makes delicacy the same forgetful thing as health.

The Apostle traces this power of sin to torment, to the law. He means any law and all law. Law is what forbids and threatens; law bears gallingly on those who wish to break it. St. Paul declares that no law, not even God's, can make man righteous in heart. It can only force out into rebellion the sin that is in them. It is so with a nation's law. If against the spirit of the whole people there is first the murmur of disapprobation, then transgression, and then the bursting asunder of that law in national revolution. So with God's law. It will never long control a man who does not love it. First comes the sense of constraint, then a murmuring of the heart, and last the rising of passion in its giant might, made desperate by restraint. That is the law giving strength to sin.

II. FAITH CONQUERING IN DEATH.

There is nothing in all this world that ever led a man on to real victory but faith. Faith is that looking forward to a future with something like certainty, that raises man above the narrow feelings of the present. Even in this life he who is steadily pursuing a plan that requires some years to accomplish, is a man of more elevated character than he who is living by the day. And therefore it is that faith, and nothing but faith, gives victory in death. It is that elevation of character we get from looking steadily and forever forward till eternity becomes a real home to us; that enables us to look upon the grave, not as the great end of all, but only as something that stands between us and the end. We are conquerors of death when we are able to look beyond it.

This victory is to be *through* Christ. Mere victory over death is no unearthly thing. Only let a man sin desperately and long enough to shut judgment out of his creed, and he can bid defiance to death. An infidel may be, in this sense, a conqueror over death. Or mere manhood may give us a victory. We have steel and nerve enough in our hearts to dare anything. Felons die on the scaffold like men; soldiers can be hired for a few pence a day, to front death every day. Then, again, necessity makes a man the conqueror. When a man feels that he must go, he lays him down to die as a tired traveller wraps himself in his cloak to sleep. But the Christian's victory over death is different from all these.

1. *He is a conqueror over doubt.* There are some men who have never believed enough to doubt; some who have never thrown their hopes with such earnestness on the world to come as to feel any anxiety for fear it should not all be true. But every one who knows what faith is knows too what the desolation of doubt is. We pray till we begin to ask, Is there any one who hears, or am I whispering to myself? We hear the consolation administered to the bereaved, and we see the coffin lowered into the grave, and the thought comes, What if all this doctrine of a life to come be but a dream of man's imaginative mind, carried on from age to age, and so believed because it is a venerable superstition? Now Christ gives us victory over that doubt by His own resurrection. The grave has once, and more than once, given up its dead at His bidding. It is a world-fact that all the metaphysics about impossibility cannot rob us of. It means that we shall live again. Then we get the victory over doubt by living in Christ. All doubt comes from living out of habits of affectionate obedience to God. By idleness, by neglected prayer, we lose our power of realizing things not seen. Doubts can only be dispelled by that kind of active life that realizes Christ. When such a man comes near the vault, it is no world of sorrows he is entering. He is only going to see things that he has felt, for he

has been living in heaven. He has his grasp on things other men are only groping after, and touching now and then.

2. *He is a conqueror over fear.* Let us understand what really is the victory over the fear of death. It may be rapture, or it may not. That depends very much on the temperament; and, after all, the broken words of a dying man are a very poor index of his real state before God. Rapturous hope has been granted to martyrs in peculiar moments. But it fosters a dangerous feeling to take such cases as precedents. Christian bravery is a deep, calm thing, unconscious of itself. There are more triumphant death-beds than we think, if we only remember this: true fearlessness makes no parade. Oh! it is not only in those passionate effusions in which the ancient martyrs spoke sometimes of panting for the crushing of their limbs by the lions in the amphitheatre, or of holding out their arms to embrace the flames that were to curl around them — it is not then only that Christ has stood by His servants and made them more than conquerors. There may be something of earthly excitement in all that. Every day his servants are dying modestly and peacefully, not a word of victory on their lips, but Christ's deep triumph in their hearts, watching the slow progress of their decay, yet so far emancipated from personal anxiety that they are still able to think and plan for others, not knowing that they are doing any great thing. They come to the battle-field to which they have been looking forward all their lives, and there is no foe with which to fight.

3. *He gains the victory by his resurrection.* It is a rhetorical expression rather than sober truth when we call anything but the resurrection victory over death. We may conquer doubt and fear, but that is not conquering dying. It is like a warrior crushed to death by a superior antagonist, refusing to yield a groan, and bearing the glance of defiance to the last. And when you see flesh melting away, and mental power becoming infantine in its feebleness, and lips scarcely able to articulate, is there left for a moment a doubt as to who is the conqueror?

Bear in mind what this world would be without the thought of a resurrection. If we could conceive an unselfish man looking on this world of desolation with that infinite compassion which all the brave and good feel, what conception could he have but that of defeat, failure — the sons of man mounting into a bright existence, and one after another falling back into darkness and nothingness, like soldiers trying to mount an impracticable breach, and falling back crushed and mangled into the ditch before the bayonets and rattling fire of their conquerors. Until a man looks on evil till it seems like a real personal enemy rejoicing over the destruction it has made, he can scarcely conceive Paul's rapture when he remembered all this to be reversed, when this sad world is to put off *forever* its changefulness and misery, the grave is to be robbed of its victory, and the bodies are to come forth purified by their long sleep. One battle has been fought by Christ, and another battle, most real and difficult, but a conquering one, is to be fought by us. — FREDERICK W. ROBERTSON.

LESSONS FROM LIFE'S BREVITY (Ps. 90:12)

No difference is so wide as that existing between life and death. In the activities of the one and the stillness of the other, the familiar tones of life and the unnatural hush of death, is manifest an incongruity more painful than is anywhere else observed. The stillness of death renders the occasion a time favorable for hearkening to those echoes which respond to the questionings of the heart. Death brings its sadness, if not its gloom; but even this reveals a light precious and cheering.

The questionings of the intellect are important, yet its responses at such a time are necessarily evasive. The giants of thought can be observed then but as gladiators which struggle in the arena for the mastery. From such curious displays men turn away to listen to the heart's throbs. They are not cold and distant, nor abstruse and evasive. The schools of philosophy may hide their evidences in the alcoves of learning beyond the reach of the masses, but the heart writes, in lines of light and shadings of sorrow, a vernacular which can be read by all. The masses may not be able to define life, but they feel its throbs. They may not trace the threads of its intricate logic, but they can feel the assurance of its unmistakable impressions, as Mrs. Browning says:

> "Like a white soul tossed out to eternity
> With the thrills of time upon it."

It is then, when the death shadow has fallen about our path, that we are impressed with

I. THE BREVITY OF LIFE. Brevity is a relative term. To the child who anticipates a coming pleasure, the lagging hours are torture with their delay. To the child who has entered into the possession of the coveted delight, the hour is gone as though its minutes were but moments. To the aged man, boyhood is crowded into a distant perspective, while to the same, life yesterday was as the flight of time. But if the heart is caught in the cruel cogs of sorrow, the moment is as an hour, and the hour becomes an age. But when the soul stands where it surveys in dread or hope the vast stretches of the future, time is relegated to its appropriate brief curve in the swift current of being.

Time is but a speck, the merest dot along the ages. What is the age of a man compared with that of the race, and this with the vast stretch of world-building which stretches from Eden back to "the beginning"? It was such a retrospect which moved Jacob to declare in the presence of Egypt's King: "The days of the years of my pilgrimage are an hundred and thirty years: few and evil have the days of the years of my life been."

The brevity of life is forcibly suggested by Moses in this nine-tieth Psalm. It is as a flood which rises upon the impulse of weeping skies, which threatens to be a permanent devastation, and yet in a single night retires within its banks and promises obediently to minister to the beauty of nature and the welfare of man. It is also as a sleep. Who does not know the sweetness of sleep in the years preceding the weight of care? The child weary with play sinks to his pillow, and is only aroused by the advance of the brightening morning, to question the assertion that night is equal in length to the day. And so is life, a brief, dreamless sleep.

Again, says the Psalmist, "We spend our years as a tale that is told." From parental lips we heard the recital of childish story. It was the delight of only the fraction of an hour, and the tale was told. And such is life. Notwithstanding its engrossing interests of business and amusement, soon it is gone, even as a tale that is told. The moment refuses to stay and rushes with its impress of virtue or of sin into the unchangeable past. The grass, too, in its fragile beauty, is made to illustrate this same all-important truth. Mark its tender growth and speedy maturity. "In the morning it flourisheth and groweth up," but the instruction is in its speedy decay; for "in the evening it is cut down and withereth. For the sun is no sooner risen with a burning heat, but it withereth the grass, and the flower thereof falleth, and the grace of the fashion of it perisheth." All flesh is grass, and all the goodliness thereof is as the flower of the field." So whether we wake or sleep, work or pray, we grow in days and in years, and — then die.

II. THE VANITY OF EARTHLY PURSUITS. The masses by their action seem to indicate that they expect to live here forever. The foundations of their mansions of pleasure are deep and strong, the walls thick and high, as though they were to shelter the millenarian instead of the man of threescore years and ten.

One large part of humanity are busy with the effort to accumulate riches, as though this were the chief end of man. They heap up riches as though they knew who should father them. Another part, goaded by a conscienceless ambition, are reaching after worldly distinction. The most tender and fragrant vines of the soul are ruthlessly trampled under foot, that they may send a sounding name abroad, only to make at the last the fearful discovery that ambition's highest success is the soul's deepest delusion. Wolsey said: "If I had served my God with half that I have served my king, He would not in mine age have left me naked to mine enemies." Napoleon in bitterness of spirit saw the walls of his empire crumbling about him, though they had cost the sacrifice of myriads of lives. It were assuredly wiser to sing with a man who wore honors forced upon him:

"O why should the spirit of mortal be proud?"

Then worldly pleasures make sensuous appeals for the devotion of immortals. The world's actors are numerous and talented, its highest purpose of life. But it is only a repetition of the same mistake. The soul, true to its heavenly origin, refuses to be satisfied with the unreal fictions of the stage and the intoxicating maze of the dance. Over all may be inscribed the character, *Unsatisfying*. A Roman emperor offered a reward to the inventor of a new pleasure. His was the poet's experience:

"I have sought round this verdant earth,
    For unfading joy;
I have tried every source of mirth,
    But all, all will cloy."

Can such persons have numbered the brief moments which will so soon introduce them to that unfamiliar future, from whose bourn no traveller ever returns? If the Epicurean sentiment be true, such surrender to the waves of sensual pleasure is consistent and desirable; but if "the soul, immortal as its Sire, can never die," such indifference is reckless and reprehensible.

III. HOW CAN WE APPLY OUR HEARTS UNTO WISDOM? The chief end of man is not amusement and pleasure-seeking. These are selfish and narrowing. God places before the race a broader and more enlarging mission, in which there is a brighter glory and a truer happiness. "The chief end of man is to honor and glorify God, and to enjoy Him forever." Living is full of terrible responsibilities. No wonder they overawed the majestic minds of Kant and Webster! It is the mind unable or disinclined to sweep the wide vista of destiny that drifts aimlessly, as though a bright destiny were without conditions. But everywhere success attends studied preparation, while failure follows in the wake of indifference. Life has placed its secular prizes beyond reach of the listless and indifferent. Appreciation of good pays the price of effort for its attainment. This means a hand on the helm, an arm at the oar, an eye on the chart, while the anchor awaits an emergency. God very wisely placed the glory of mind at the goal of intelligent investigation. Study is the mind's stimulus, and achievement its greatest joy. And the same divine goodness would reveal any essential truth, which by its nature was beyond man's powers of discovery. And yet with all their studying, ancient sages only guessed at moral truth. Here they needed that one who knew its influence, without the delays and disappointments of experiment, should announce what was beyond, and how, if desirable, it might be attained. David felt the need. Destiny was crowding him, and he knew not in the darkness where to place his feet, till the wave of a mysterious wand made a rift in the overshadowing mist. Then in his joy he cried out, "Thou wilt guide me with thy counsel, and afterward receive me to glory." God's counsel expresses His will, and is therefore good, perfect, and acceptable. This life with its varied experiences cannot disclose the wisdom of this will; but as the soul among the possible ten thousand plans finds the one which shines brighter and brighter even to the perfect day; as from the eternal heights it regards the wisdom of God's plan disclosed, it will join a chorus of the saved in ascribing wisdom to Him whom we should serve. Moore caught a glimpse of this peerless wisdom:

> "Go wing your flight from star to star,
> From world to shining world, as far
>   As the universe spreads its flaming wall
> Count all the pleasures of all the spheres,
> And multiply each by thousands of years:
>   One moment in heaven is worth them all."
>   — W. W. RAMSAY.

THE MASTER'S CALL IN AFFLICTION (John 11:28)

Why not sooner? Mary might naturally have asked. Day after day she and Martha had awaited his approach. But now all was over. Lazarus was dead and buried. Of what avail Christ's coming now? The language was, "If thou hadst been here, my brother had not died." And so we reason in our moments of despair, when our prayers are not answered in the way we desired, when our friends are not restored to health, and God's presence is not felt. But not so Mary. She arose quickly and came unto Him, believing He had done all things well. God never sends bereavement into a Christian family without some special end in view. As in this case, the end may not at the time be apparent, but we may rest assured He doth not willingly afflict the children of men.

I. THE MASTER CALLS US TO COMMUNE WITH HIM.

Mary had often before this sat at the feet of Christ; but that was in the days when no sickness or deep sorrow afflicted the household, when there was no special call to muse upon the lessons of mortality. All this is now changed. Alone with Christ, she must be taught the reasons for God's mysterious dealings with her, be taught to bow to His will. The Master called her to impart such knowledge as she had never yet learned, nor could learn but in the closest communion such as sorrow gives.

So it is with every Christian. While he enjoys communion with Christ in every season of existence, yet there are times when he must withdraw from the common surroundings, and be alone with Christ. Mary must leave Martha behind when she would commune with Jesus at such seasons. How often amid the cares of everyday life secret communion is neglected! Yet how we murmur at the sudden calamity that summons us to closer fellowship with God! How few of us take time to examine our hearts, and review our lives, except when laid on a sick-bed, or when beside the grave of a friend! And even then the lesson is soon forgot, as the world's cares again occupy our minds. But when death invades our own home, when the cradle is emptied, or the son or daughter of blessed promise is snatched from us, or the husband or wife is taken from the center of the home, then we feel there is only one with whom we can converse. "The Master has come, and calleth for thee."

II. THE MASTER CALLS US TO EXPERIENCE HIS SYMPATHY AND RECEIVE DIVINE CONSOLATION.

Mary and Martha were not without sympathizing friends; but there come times when any sympathy is an intrusion. Christ did not come at the moment of bereavement; he waited purposely till several days had elapsed. But a period comes when the heart yearns for companionship. We would not undervalue the real sympathies of Christian friends, but above all we would have the companionship of Jesus himself. He knows us as no other can; his love surpasses all earthly love. And though we cannot hear him face to face, as did Mary, he still speaks to us through the Comforter, and in the words of revelation.

III. THE MASTER CALLS US TO BEHOLD GREATER REVELATIONS OF HIS POWER AND GOODNESS.

Martha looked forward with hope to the last resurrection; but Christ designs gifts of mercy for these sorrowing sisters far beyond their expectations. Such a manifestation of his power as he soon displayed, they had never, in all these years, before seen. Though for us he does not restore our dead, yet he teaches us to regard them as not dead but living. The mere possibility of eternal separation will haunt even the Christian's mind: but Christ aids us to overmaster all doubts and fears.

IV. TO EACH OF US IT WILL BE SAID SOME TIME, "THE MASTER IS COME, AND CALLETH FOR THEE."

To some that call will come at the hour of death, and it may come at any time. To some it may come at the Second Advent. But to all it will come at the Day of Judgment. To many, come whenever it may, it will be sudden and unexpected. Are we prepared for it? Are our calling and election sure?

Business men at certain seasons balance their accounts, examine the true state of their affairs. Have we settled the accounts with our Maker? Have we during the past year improved the many privileges God has given us? Have we availed ourselves of the means of grace? Have we made attainments in holiness? What have we done for humanity, for God's glory, for advancing His cause during the year? To many families in this Church the Master's call has come this year; but it should be heard by all. We cannot tell who may next be called into the presence of the Judge. — WILLIAM COCHRANE.

III. Funeral Sermons and Outlines

DEATH OF BELIEVERS (Rom. 8:10, 11)

I. Why does death pass upon the body of the Christian?
   A. The body is the instrument through which we sin, and a provocative to sin.
   B. It is not the design of grace to remove evil out of the world, but to convert it into a means of discipline.
   C. The body must die that, by being sanctified, it may be fitted for the world of glory.
   D. The sudden translation of believers would subvert the principle of grace.
   E. The translation of believers would anticipate the Judgment Day.

II. Why is the body to be raised again?
   A. The body will be raised because it is equally with the soul redeemed by Christ and united to him.
      1. The body, as a constituent part of us, must be as truly redeemed as the soul.
      2. Christ assumed human nature, body as well as soul, and we are united to him in both. (See Rom. 6:5; I Cor. 15:20; Eph. 5:30.)
      3. The curse of sin has fallen upon the body as well as upon the soul, equally necessitating its redemption. (See Gen. 3:16-18; Rom. 8:23.)
      4. The Scriptures bear special testimony to the redemption of the body, and to its union with Christ. (See Isa. 26:19; Rom. 1:3, 4; 8:19, 23; Eph. 5:30; I Cor. 6:15.)
   B. The body will be raised because of the indwelling of the Holy Ghost.
      1. Because it is the Holy Ghost's prerogative to impart life.
      2. The Holy Ghost is the bond by which the believer is united with Jesus Christ.

3. The body of the saint is the temple of the Holy Ghost. (I Cor. 3:16, 17; 6:19; II Cor. 6:16.)

4. The Holy Spirit is the sanctifier, and by virtue of this office will raise the bodies of them that sleep in Jesus.

— B. M. PALMER.

THE DEATH OF A MOTHER (Ps. 35:14)

I. A mother's death reminds us of the blessings conferred by God through the maternal relation.

II. The death of a mother occasions bitter recollections of filial disobedience and neglect.

III. It breaks up the home of our early days, and makes us feel we are only sojourners here.

IV. The death of a mother, especially of an aged mother, makes us sensible of our nearness to another world.
   A. I appeal to fathers.
   B. I appeal to mothers.
   C. I appeal to those whose mother is living.
   D. I appeal to those whose mother is dead.

— JOHN M. JOHNSON.

DEATH IN THE MIDST OF LIFE (Jer. 15:9)

I. The sun in its splendor.

   A. *Its natural glory.* The most glorious of the heavenly bodies, it well typifies moral excellence and spiritual glory. (See II Cor. 3:18.)

   B. *Its constancy.* The center of the solar system, many times larger than the earth, it stands forth as the most sublime of God's material works. How constantly, without interruption or decrease, it is fulfilling the purpose of its Creator! What destruction would result from irregularity in the exertion of its power! So with the Christian. (See I Cor. 4:9.)

   C. *Its influence.* Of how much beauty and comfort are its rays the source! Without them life were impossible, and the earth a sterile, uninhabitable mass. Such is every spot where the Christian life is unknown. All the blessings of civilization flow from the Sun of Righteousness. "Ye are the lights of the world," etc.

II. The setting sun.

    A. *The certainty of its setting.* As certain is death.

    B. *The diversity in the time of its setting.* We have the short day of winter, the long day of summer. But still more diverse is the period of life. How often does its sun go down while it is yet day!

    C. *The frequent beauty of its setting.* "Let me die the death of the righteous, and let my last end be like his."

    D. *The sun sets to shine upon another horizon.*

JABEZ BURNS.

SUDDEN DEATH: IS IT TO BE DEPRECATED?
(Ps. 90:12)

I. The uncertain duration of life.

    A. *The high pressure of modern life increases this uncertainty.* Overtaxed hearts and brains yield suddenly, and the frail thread of life snaps as tow when touched by the flame.

    B. *The illustrations abound on all sides.* To no community are sudden deaths unknown. On all sides we see strong men suddenly stricken.

    C. *It should alter our standard of value of men.* The uncertainty in the time of death involves the instability of the most brilliant talents and richest possessions. What a man has is too often the standard of worth, while a man is living; what he has done, is the ultimate standard of the world; what he has been, is God's standard.

II. Why sudden death should be deprecated.

    A. *It inflicts anguish upon the living.*

    B. *We need the lessons taught us from sick-beds.* The prayers, the counsel, the exhortations of the dying have brought many to the cross. Christ is brought nearer in suffering.

    C. *It deprives those unprepared for death, of a last chance of repentance.*

— EDWARD CAPEL CURE.

THE LORD'S SHEEP IN THE VALLEY OF THE
SHADOW OF DEATH (Ps. 23:4)
 I. Guided by the shepherd.
    A. The shepherd has a wise purpose in doing this.
    B. The shepherd chooses the valleys himself.
    C. The shepherd goes before his sheep.
 II. Surrounded by dangers.
    A. There are serious dangers in these valleys.
    B. The shepherd knows all dangers. .
    C. He averts these dangers.
III. Sustained by faith.
    A. Faith makes the sheep willing to follow.
    B. Faith removes fear of evil.
    C. Faith comforts with the guidance of the shepherd.
                                        — W. P. VAN WYK.

THE DARKNESS OF PROVIDENCE (John 13:7)
 I. Reasons for the mystery of God's dispensations.
    A. It is necessary to the assertion of God's absolute suprem-
       acy.
    B. This darkness rests upon Providence because of its com-
       plexity.
    C. The violence of our emotions renders us incompetent to
       understand.
    D. Our spiritual state is often inadequate to receive the ex-
       planation.
    E. The great law of faith renders this mystery indispensable.
 II. This mystery of God's providences will be temporary.
    A. There is a strong presumption that this revelation will be
       made in the known connection between the two worlds.
    B. All limitations of sense will be removed.
    C. God's plans there will be complete.
    D. The removal of this obscurity is necessary to God's vin-
       dication.
    E. Heaven is the state and place of reward and praise.
                                        —B. M. PALMER.

THE LORD WEIGHETH THE HEART (Prov. 21:2b)
 I. The Lord is an infallible weigher of hearts.
    A. A warning lesson for unscrupulous people.
    B. A comforting lesson for scrupulous people.

II. The Lord is an authoritative weigher of hearts.
    A. The Lord alone is authoritative.
    B. Man of self is not an authoritative weigher.

III. The Lord is a just weigher of hearts.
    A. What does the Lord put in the scales?
    B. What do the Lord's scales indicate then?
    C. What is the result of this weighing?
                  — W. P. Van Wyk.

THE HEAVENLY WORLD (Rev. 21:25)

    I. There is no night of ignorance in heaven.
    II. No night of error in heaven.
    III. No night of sin in heaven.
    IV. No night of conflict in heaven.
    V. No night of weariness in heaven.
    VI. No night of danger in heaven.
    VII. No night of sorrow in heaven.
    VIII. No night of suffering in heaven.
    IX. Finally, there is no night of death in heaven.
                  —J. M. Sherwood.

IV. Illustrations and Quotations

CERTAINTY OF DEATH

There is nothing more certain than death, nothing more uncertain than the time of dying. — WARWICK.

DEATH, A CHANGE OF PLACE ONLY

If I am taken out of the world, I shall only change my place: I shall neither change my company nor my communion.

— THOMAS SHEPPARD.

DEATH OF CHILDREN

The good husbandman may pluck his roses and gather in his lilies at midsummer, and for aught I daresay in the beginning of the first summer month; and he may transplant young trees out of the lower ground to the higher, where they have more of the sun, and a more free air at any season of the year. What is that to you or me? The goods are his own. — RUTHERFORD.

CONDITION OF AN EASY DEATH

He dies easily who feels that Christ died for him.

EARLY DEATH

"I spare none," saith Death. Man's life is but a day, a short day, a winter's day. Ofttimes the sun goes down upon a man before it be well up. Your day is short, your work is great, your journey long, and, therefore, you should rise early, and set forward towards heaven betimes, as that man doth that hath a long journey to go in a winter's day. — BROOKS.

EMPTY HANDS IN DEATH

I remember an Eastern legend which I have always thought furnished a remarkable though unconscious commentary on the words of the Psalmist. Alexander the Great, we are there told, being upon his death-bed, commanded that when he was carried forth to the grave his hands should not be wrapped as was usual in the cere-cloths, but should be left outside the bier, so that all might see them, and might see that they were empty, that there

was nothing in them; that he, born to one empire, and the conqueror of another, the possessor while he lived of two worlds —
of the East and of the West — and of the treasures of both, yet
now when he was dead could retain no smallest portion of these
treasures; that in this matter the poorest beggar and he were at
length upon equal terms. — Trench.

DEATH EVERYWHERE
And all this is the law and constitution of nature; it is a punishment to our sins, the unalterable event of Providence, and the
decree of heaven; the chains that confine us to this condition are
as strong as destiny, and immutable as the eternal laws of God.
—Jeremy Taylor.

> "With heavenly weapons he has fought
>   The battles of his Lord,
> Finished his course, and kept the faith,
>   And gained the great reward."—Stevens.

PARTING OF DEATH
A minister called upon another, then upon his dying bed. As
they shook hands at parting, the latter said, "Brother, we part at
the footstool, we shall meet again at the throne."

PICTURE OF DEATH
What I am when death is held before me, that I must be forever. When my spirit departs, if God finds me hymning his
praise, I shall hymn it in heaven; if he finds me breathing out
oaths, I shall follow up those oaths in hell. — Spurgeon.

PREPARATION FOR DEATH
Death is never sudden to a saint; no guest comes unawares to
him who keepeth a constant table; but as when the ray dawns
to us in Europe, the shadows of the evening are stretched on
Asia, so the day of their redemption will be a long night of destruction to thee. — Swinnock.

PUTTING OFF THE THOUGHT OF DEATH
Is it not then, think you, a great folly that men are so unwill-
ing to think of death? The mariner with joy thinks of the haven:
the laborer is glad to see the evening: the soldier is not sorry
when his warfare is accomplished: and shall we be grieved when
the days of sin are ended? — Hill.

QUESTIONS OF DEATH

Rev. John Newton one day mentioned in company the death of a lady. A young woman who sat opposite immediately said, "O sir, how did she die?" The clergyman replied, "There is a more important question than that, my dear, which you should have asked first." "Sir," said she, "what question can be more important than 'How did she die?'" "How did she live?" was Mr. Newton's answer.

PICTURE OF DEATH

In a scantily furnished chamber lies an old Scotch minister with thin gray hair, and wrinkled skin. But his brow is high and broad; his deep-set eyes are bright and piercing; a smile plays round his lips; and though feeble and dying, he looks calm and happy. Let us speak to him and say: "Do you think yourself dying, dear sir?" He fixes his eye calmly upon you, and slowly he replies: "Really, friend, I am not anxious whether I am or not; for if I die, I shall be with God; if I live, He will be with me." — PROTESTANT CHURCHMAN.

DEATH, UNLOOKED FOR

Quevedo asks, "How can death be sudden to a being who always knew that he must die, and that the time of his death was uncertain?"

DEATH

Common as life is, death, its counterpart, though less apparent, is not less common. As if it were the shadow which life casts upon the ground, there, along with it, goes that dark, unsocial, dumb companion. For though not coeval, death is coexistent with life; so that wherever you find the one in this world, you find the other. — T. GUTHRIE, D.D.

DEATH IN OLD AGE

It is not less natural for the old to die than for the fields to mellow in autumn, or for the fruit when ripe to fall from the tree. And who would repine that the weary pilgrim reaches his journey's end — that the worn-out traveller gets to a resting-place — or that the mariner, after a long and boisterous voyage, gains a haven of perpetual repose? — GEMS OF THOUGHT.

IMPARTIALITY OF DEATH
One may live as a conqueror, a king, or a magistrate; but he must die as a man. —D. WEBSTER.

THE LIFE THAT PREPARES FOR DEATH
If life has not made you by God's grace, through faith, holy — think you, will death without faith do it? The cold waters of that narrow stream are no purifying bath in which you may wash and be clean. No! no! as you go down into them, you will come up from them. — REV. A. MACLAREN, D.D.

He who cannot think cheerfully of death has probably never thought cheerfully and rationally of life. To those to whom death is a mysterious, and therefore repugnant image, life itself can be little more than a confused riddle; for they cannot, as yet, have any clear conception of the purpose of their existence.

— LSCHOKKE.

A SIMILE OF DEATH
God's finger touched him, and he slept. — LORD TENNYSON.

RESURRECTION
The fact of the resurrection, and not its mode, receives chief emphasis in the New Testament. *The fact is certain,* and it is portrayed constantly as a spiritual experience and process.

— WILLIAM HANNA

IMMORTALITY
The dead are the living. They lived while they died; and after they die, they live on forever. — DR. MACLAREN.

THE FUTURE LIFE
An old Scotchman, while dying, was asked what he thought of death, and he replied, "It matters little to me whether I live or die. If I die I will be with Jesus, and, if I live Jesus will be with me."

Some time ago a man of large property died, and I asked a friend, "How much did he leave?" I was somewhat startled when he answered, "All of it, Sir, he didn't take a cent with him." He went out of the world as poor as when he entered it.

Moody's last words are familiar to all: "I see earth receding, heaven is opening; God is calling me."

Among the dying sayings of the heavenly-minded David Brainerd, President Edwards has recorded the following: "My heaven is to please God, and to glorify him, and give all to him, and to be wholly devoted to his glory; that is my religion and that is my happiness, and always was ever since I supposed I had any true religion; and all those that are of that religion shall meet me in heaven. I do not go to heaven to be advanced, but to give honor to God. It is no matter where I shall be stationed in heaven whether I have a high or a low seat there, but to love and please and glorify God is all."

"Christians never see each other for the last time. — Adieu!" said the German Princess, Maria Dorothea, as she bade farewell to a parting missionary.

At death the Christian simply crosses the summit of the earthly life, and lives on a sunnier side, whilst our poor sight stops with the intervening line of hills. — ROBERT F. SAMPLE, D.D.

Too little do we, in the rivalries and anxieties of our human life permit the blessed influences of that holy world to allure and to occupy us.

THE CHRISTIAN LIFE

A noble Christian man lay dying. His pastor asked him: "Are you willing it shall come out just as God wills, your life to go out or to stay here?" and he answered: "Of course. I have no use for my life but to serve the will of God with it." That was the answer of a crown prince. He was God's own son. He accepted God's will and lived to God's glory.

DEATH

It is said of the celebrated Caesar Borgia, that in his last moments he exclaimed: "I have provided, in the course of my life, *for everything except death;* and now, alas! I am to die, although entirely unprepared."

A consumptive disease seized the eldest son and heir of the Duke of Hamilton, which ended in his death. A little while before his death, he took the Bible from under his pillow, and read several comforting passages. As death approached, he called his younger brother to his bedside, and after talking affectionately and seriously to him, closed with these words: "And now, Douglas, in a little while you'll be a duke, but I shall be a king."

— W. R. CLARK.

Death levels master and slave, the sceptre and the law and makes the unlike like. — WALTER COLMAN.

The tall, the wise, the reverend head, Must lie as low as ours.
— WATTS.

He that would die well must always look for death, every day knocking at the gates of the grave; and then the gates of the grave shall never prevail upon him to do him mischief.
— JEREMY TAYLOR.

Death borders upon our birth; and our cradle stands in our grave. — BISHOP HALL.

V. Quotable Poetry

ONLY A FEW MORE YEARS

A few more years shall roll,
  A few more seasons come,
And shall be with those that rest,
  Asleep within the tomb;
  Then, O my Lord, prepare
  My soul for that great day;
Oh, wash me in Thy precious Blood,
  And take my sins away.

A few more storms shall beat
  On this wild rocky shore,
And we shall be where tempests cease,
  And surges swell no more:
  Then, O my Lord, prepare
  My soul for that calm day;
Oh, wash me in Thy precious Blood,
  And take my sins away.

A few more suns shall set
  O'er these dark hills of time
And we shall be where suns are not,
  A far serener clime;
  Then, O my Lord, prepare
  My soul for that bright day;
Oh, wash me in Thy precious Blood,
  And take my sins away.

A few more struggles here,
  A few more partings o'er,
A few more toils, a few more tears,
  And we shall weep no more:
  Then, O my Lord, prepare
  My soul for that blest day;
Oh, wash me in Thy precious Blood,
  And take my sins away.

— HORATIO BONAR

THE HOUR OF DEATH

Leaves have their time to fall
And flowers to wither at the north-wind's breath
And stars to set — but all,
Thou hast all seasons for thine own, O Death!
— FELICIA HEMANS.

LOVE'S CHASTENINGS

When thou hast thanked thy God for every blessing
sent,
What time will then remain for murmurs or lament?
When God afflicts thee, think He hews a rugged
stone,
Which must be shaped, or else aside as useless
thrown. — RICHARD CHENEVIX TRENCH, D.D.

THE ROD

O Thou whose sacred feet have trod
The thorny path of woe,
Forbid that I should slight the rod
Or faint beneath the blow.

Give me the spirit of Thy trust,
To suffer as a son;
To say, though lying in the dust,
Father; Thy will be done! — J. D. BURNS.

THE DAILY PRAISE

O, what is life?
A toil, a strife,
Were it not lighted by thy love divine.
I ask not wealth,
I crave not health:
Living or dying, Lord, I would be thine!
O, what is death
When the poor breath
In parting can the soul to thee resign?
While patient love
Her trust doth prove,
Living or dying, Lord, I would be thine!

Throughout my days,
Be constant praise
Uplift to thee from out this heart of mine;
So shall I be
Brought nearer thee;
Living or dying, Lord, I would be thine!

— FENELON.

IT IS NOT DEATH TO DIE

It is not death to die,
To leave this weary road,
And midst the brotherhood on high
To be at home with God.

It is not death to close
The eye long dimmed by tears,
And wake in glorious repose
To spend eternal years.

It is not death to bear
The stroke that sets us free
From earthly chain, to breathe the air
Of boundless liberty.

It is not death to fling
Aside this mortal dust,
And rise on strong exulting wing
To live among the just.

Giver and Lord of life!
In thee we cannot die;
Grant us to conquer in the strife,
And dwell with thee on high.

— H. A. CESAR MALAN.

THOUGHTS ON DEATH

The stream is calmest when it nears the tide,
And flowers are sweetest at the eventide,
And birds most musical at close of day,
And saints divinest when they pass away.

Morning is lovely, but a holier charm
Lies folded close in Evening's robe of balm;
And weary man must ever love her best,
For Morning calls to toil, but Night to rest.

She comes from heaven, and on her wings doth bear
A holy fragrance, like the breath of prayer;
Footsteps of angels follow in her trace,
To shut the weary eyes of day in peace.

O, when our sun is setting, may we glide
Like summer's evening down the golden tide,
And leave behind us, as we pass away,
Sweet, starry twilight round our sleeping clay!

— ANON

JESUS LIVES

Jesus lives! thy terrors now
  Can no longer , death, appall us;
Jesus lives! by this we know
    Thou, O grave, canst not enthrall us.
    Alleluia!

Jesus lives! henceforth is death
  But the gate of life immortal;
This shall calm our trembling breath,
    When we pass its gloomy portal.
    Alleluia!

— CHRISTIAN F. GELLERT.

I CANNOT THINK OF THEM AS DEAD

I cannot think of them as dead
  Who walk with me no more;
Along the path of life I tread
  They have but gone before.

The Father's house is mansioned fair
  Beyond my vision dim;
All souls are his, and here or there
  Are living unto him.

And still their silent ministry
    Within my heart hath place
As when on earth they walked with me
    And met me face to face.

Their lives are made forever mine;
    What they to me have been
Hath left henceforth its seal and sign
    Engraven deep within.

Mine are they by an ownership
    Nor time nor death can free;
For God hath given to love to keep
    Its own eternally.

                — FREDERICK L. HOSMER.

ETERNAL LIFE

Though home be dear, and life be sweet,
And thankful hearts God's bounty greet,
Yet rings at times the message clear
'Our soul's true city is not here.'

'Mid changing scenes of joy and pain,
There comes, again and yet again,
A vision of the changeless rest,
Where God's own face shall make us blest.

And through the web of earthly life,
Its grief and gladness, work and strife,
There runs a thread divine, to tie
Our time-life to the life on high.

O help us, Lord, with thankful heart
To grasp each day's eternal part,
And build our home on that calm height
Where saints do walk with thee in light.

                — ELLA S. ARMITAGE.

ABIDE WITH ME

Abide with me; fast falls the eventide;
The darknness deepens; Lord, with me abide!
When other helpers fail, and comforts flee,
Help of the helpless, O abide with me!

Swift to its close ebbs out life's little day:
Earth's joys grow dim, its glories pass away;
Change and decay in all around I see;
O thou who changest not, abide with me!

I need thy presence ev'ry passing hour;
What but thy grace can foil the tempter's power?
Who, like thyself, my guide and stay can be?
Thro' cloud and sunshine, Lord, abide with me!

I fear no foe, with thee at hand to bless;
Ills have no weight, and tears no bitterness;
Where is death's sting? where, grave, thy victory!
I triumph still, if thou abide with me.

— HENRY F. LYTE

ASLEEP IN JESUS

Asleep in Jesus! blessed sleep!
From which none ever wake to weep;
A calm and undisturbed repose,
Unbroken by the last of foes.

Asleep in Jesus! Oh, how sweet
To be for such a slumber meet;
With holy confidence to sing
That death has lost its venomed sting.

Asleep in Jesus! peaceful rest!
Whose waking is supremely blest;
No fear, no woe, shall dim the hour
That manifests the Savior's pow'r.

Asleep in Jesus! far from thee
Thy kindred and their graves may be;
But thine is still a blessed sleep
From which none ever wake to weep!

— MRS. MACKAY

HOW BLEST THE RIGHTEOUS WHEN HE DIES

How blest the righteous when he dies!
When sinks a weary soul to rest!
How mildly beam the closing eyes!
How gently heaves the expiring breast!

So fades a summer cloud away;
So sinks the gale when storms are o'er;
So gently shuts the eyes of day;
So dies the wave along the shore.

A holy quiet reigns around,
A calm which life not death destroys;
And naught disturbs the peace profound
Which his unfettered soul enjoys.

Life's labor done, as sinks the clay,
Light from its load the spirit flies,
While heav'n and earth combine to say,
"How blest the righteous when he dies."

— BARBAULD.

MY JESUS AS THOU WILT

My Jesus, as thou wilt! O, may thy will be mine;
Into thy hand of love I would my all resign;
Thro' sorrow or thro' joy, Conduct me as thine own,
And help me still to say, "My Lord, thy will be done."

My Jesus, as thou wilt! Tho' seen thro' many a tear,
Let not my star of hope Grow dim or disappear;
Since thou on earth hast wept And sorrow'd oft alone,
If I must weep with thee, "My Lord, thy will be done.'"

— BENJAMIN SCHMOLKE

MY END, LORD, MAKE ME KNOW

My end, Lord, make me know,
My days, how soon they fail;
And to my thoughtful spirit show
How weak I am and frail.

To Thy eternal thought
My days are but a span;
To Thee my years appear as nought,
A breath at best is man.

O Lord, regard my fears,
And answer my request;
Turn not in silence from my tears,
But give the mourner rest.

I am a stranger here,
Dependent on Thy grace,
A pilgrim, as my fathers were,
With no abiding place.

— JOSEPH E. SWEETSER.

How shocking must thy summons be, O Death!
To him that is at ease in his possessions:
Who, counting on long years of pleasure here,
Is quite unfurnish'd for that world to come!

—BLAIR.

Beyond the shining and the shading
  I shall be soon.
Beyond the hoping and the dreading
  I shall be soon.
Love, rest and home —
Lord! tarry not, but come.

— HORATIO BONAR.

VI. Themes and Texts for Funeral Sermons

CHILDREN

1. Comfort for Bereaved Parents, "Now we see through a glass, darkly'" (I Cor. 13:12).
2. Full Surrender, "The Lord gave, and the Lord hath taken away; blessed be the name of the Lord" (Job 1:21).
3. Faded Flowers, "The grass withereth, the flower fadeth, because the spirit of the Lord bloweth upon it" (Isa. 40:7).
4. Christ Gathers His Lambs, "He shall gather the lambs with his arm, and carry them in his bosom" (Isa. 40:11).

YOUNG PEOPLE

1. Be Ye Ready, "Be ye also ready; for in such an hour as ye think not the son of man cometh" (Matt. 24:44).
2. Sleep, not Death, "The damsel is not dead, but sleepeth" (Mark 5:39).
3. Shattered Plans, "Go to now, ye that say, Today or tomorrow we will go into such a city, and continue there a year, and buy and sell, and get gain: Whereas ye know not what shall be on the morrow. For what is your life? It is even a vapour, that appeareth for a little time, and then vanisheth away" (James 4:13, 14).
4. "Thy brother shall rise again" (John 11:24).

MIDDLE AGED

1. Uncertainty of the Time of Death, "For yourselves know perfectly that the day of the Lord so cometh as a thief in the night. For when they shall say, Peace and safety: then sudden destruction cometh upon them, as travail upon a woman with child; and they shall not escape. But ye, brethren, are not in darkness, that that day should overtake you as a thief" (I Thes. 5:2-4).

2. Watch Ye, "Blessed are those servants, whom the Lord when he cometh shall find watching: . . . And if he shall come in the second watch, or come in the third watch, and find them so blessed are those servants" (Luke 12:37a, 38).

3. Broken Plans, "My days are past, my purposes are broken off, even the thoughts of my heart" (Job 17:11).

4. Death in the Midst of Life, "Her sun is gone down while it was yet day" (Jer. 15:9).

AGED PERSON

1. Ripe for the Harvest, "Thou shalt come to thy grave in a full age, like as a shock of corn cometh in his season" (Job 5:26).

2. The Blessing of a Long Life, "With long life will I satisfy him and show him my salvation" (Ps. 91:16).

3. Light at Eventide, "At evening it shall be light" (Zech. 14:7).

4. Death a Translation, "And Enoch walked with God: and he was not, for God took him" (Gen. 5:24).

GENERAL

1. Tell it to Jesus, "And his disciples came, and took up the body, and buried it, and went and told Jesus" (Matt. 14:12).

2. A Better Home, "For we know that if our earthly house of this tabernacle were dissolved, we have a building of God, an house not made with hands, eternal in the heavens (II Cor. 5:1).

3. No Night There, "For there shall be no night there" (Rev. 21:25).

4. God Knows Best, "I was dumb, I opened not my mouth; because thou didst it" (Ps. 39:9).